Landscapes of

LANZAROTE

a countryside guide
Sixth edition

Noel Rochford

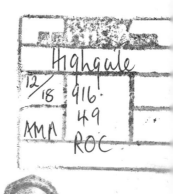

SUNFL

D1339534

Sixth edition © 2016
Sunflower Books™
PO Box 36160
London SW7 3WS, UK
www.sunflowerbooks.co.uk

ISBN 978-1-85691-460-4

Timanfaya camel train

Important note to the reader

We have tried to ensure that the descriptions and maps in this book are
error-free at press date. The book will be updated, where necessary,
whenever future printings permit. It will be very helpful for us to receive
your comments (sent in care of the publishers, please) for the updating
of future printings.

   We also rely on those who use this book — especially walkers — to
take along a good supply of common sense when they explore.
Conditions change fairly rapidly on Lanzarote, and *storm damage or
bulldozing may make a route unsafe at any time*. If the route is not as
we outline it here, and your way ahead is not secure, return to the point
of departure. *Never attempt to complete a tour or walk under hazardous
conditions!* Please read carefully the notes on pages 18 and 36-40, as
well as the introductory comments at the beginning of each tour and
walk (regarding road conditions, equipment, grade, distances and time,
etc). Explore *safely*, while at the same time respecting the beauty of the
countryside.

Cover photograph: In the Geria Valley (Car tour 2)
Title page: old farmhouse at Haría (Walks 7 and 8)

Photographs pages 2, 12, 14, 30, 41, 44, 45, 48, 52-53, 64 (left), 67,
   74, 78 (top and bottom), 82, 86, 89, 97, 102), 113, 134: the author;
   page 55: Reinhard Baumgärtner; cover and pages 22, 125: Shutter-
   stock; all other photographs: John and Pat Underwood
Maps and plans: Sunflower Books; walking maps Datum WGS84, UTM
   (28R) projection with 1km grid squares
A CIP catalogue record for this book is available from the British Library.
Printed and bound in England: Short Run Press, Exeter

Contents

3

4   Landscapes of Lanzarote

The dark picón-covered gardens of Mancha Blanca, with the yawning craters of Montaña Blanca and Caldereta in the background (Car tour 2, Walk 13)

Preface

Within just a few years, Lanzarote grew from a quiet, relatively unknown resort to an island buzzing with over a million tourists every year.

When I wrote the first edition of this book in 1989, all eyes were on this island. Would it indeed set an example in preservation, or would it follow in the footsteps of Tenerife and Gran Canaria, falling prey to the concrete of greedy developers? Fortunately, Lanzarote had one advantage over the other islands. It was the home of the well-known artist-designer — and, more importantly, conservationist — the late César Manrique. Together with his supporters, he worked to preserve the island's environmental heritage. Despite the tourist boom, they succeeded in orchestrating a well-pitched harmony between man and the landscape. As a result, in 1994 Lanzarote was declared a 'World Reserve of the Biosphere' by UNESCO — the first such award ever given to an entire island.

This fascinating 797-square-kilometre island is truly extraordinary. Its fate was decided over two and one-half centuries ago, when the largest volcanic eruption in recorded history took place, leaving a strange and alluring countryside in its wake — a landscape littered with volcanoes and dark streams of jagged lava. This is the backdrop to nearly every scene on the island, and intriguing sights abound, as you can see from the photographs in this book.

Few holidaymakers realise that Lanzarote has more to offer than just beaches and sunshine. If you were to suggest walking on Lanzarote to most visitors, they would think you mad. 'Where is there to walk?' But I can think of no better place in the Canary Islands for just strolling. No doubt 'serious' walkers will find Tenerife, La Palma and Gran Canaria, for example, more challenging, but ramblers will be in their element on Lanzarote. Each of the walks in this book takes you to a different corner of the island and shows you a scenically-different outlook. But if walking is not your favourite pastime, then *do* rent a vehicle of sorts and explore on wheels. Use the book to reach places off the beaten track and see another face of Lanzarote.

I hope that *Landscapes of Lanzarote* convinces you that there is much more to the island than beaches and sunshine.

NOEL ROCHFORD

Acknowledgements

I am greatly indebted to the following organisations for their help with the preparation of the first few editions of this book: the Patronato Insular de Turismo de Lanzarote; the island Government (Cabildo de Lanzarote), the Spanish Army's Cartographic Service in Madrid (Servicio Geográfico del Ejército), and the National Institute for the Environment (ICONA).

For the revision of later editions, very special thanks to Conny Spelbrink and my publisher Pat Underwood, who revised all the tours and walks for the Fifth edition and this Sixth edition. Thanks also to the correspondents who originally contributed Walks 11 and 31, and indeed to all the users who write to us with Updates for our website.

Useful website/books

www.lanzarote.com

Bramwell, D and Bramwell, Z: *Wild Flowers of the Canary Islands*. Stanley Thornes Ltd.

Araña, Vicente and Carracedo, Juan Carlos: *Los volcanes de las Islas Canarias, II: Lanzarote y Fuerteventura* (with English text). Editorial Rueda; available in bookshops on the island.

If you enjoy using this book, I've written several other 'Landscapes' for the Canaries: *Tenerife (Orotava • Anaga • Teno • Cañadas); La Gomera and Southern Tenerife; La Palma and El Hierro; Gran Canaria; Fuerteventura* (all published by Sunflower Books).

PUERTO DEL CARMEN

1 Tourist information	4 buses	7 Centro Comercial Biosfera	B→ Tías, San Bartolomé
2 Post office	5 clinic	A→ Airport, Arrecife	C→ Puerto Calero, Mácher, Yaiza
3 Police	6 shopping centres		

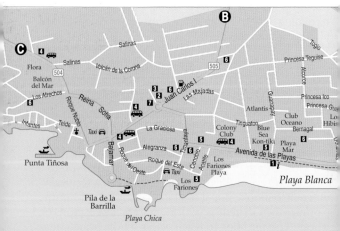

Getting about

The best way to get around Lanzarote is by **hired car**. This can be very economical, especially when you hire a car for a few days or a week. **Taxis** (only economical if shared) use meters for all journeys, even long-distance, so make sure the meter is on! Never leave anything of value in a car. Lock your belongings in the boot, or carry them with you. Thefts from cars are not uncommon. Try to park where there are other cars and people are about.

Coach tours are easy to arrange and get you to all the tourist points of interest, but never off the beaten track.

The **local bus service** is improving by leaps and bounds. Most of the walks in this book *can* be reached by bus, but you may need to travel via Arrecife. Selected bus timetables are shown on page 135, but you may find more convenient lines operating from your resort: **check the timetables at www.intercitybuslanzarote.es.** This is an excellent website, in English, which even shows all the bus lines overlaid on Google maps *with bus stops!* At press date there was no fare-saving 'bono' ticket, as there is on some other islands in the archipelago, but there *are* some reduced price tickets mentioned on the website, so you should be able to get at least 10% off normal fares by buying your ticket before boarding. See town plans below and on pages 8 and 9 *for bus stops and stations.*

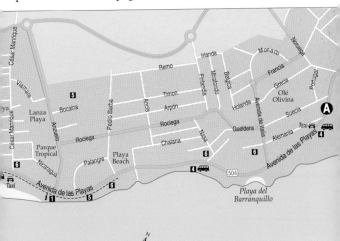

PUERTO DEL CARMEN

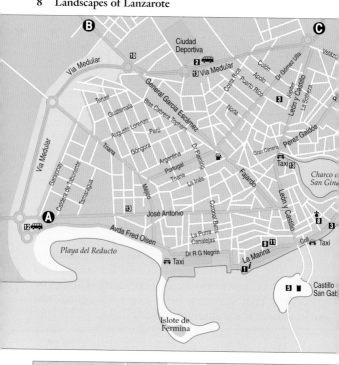

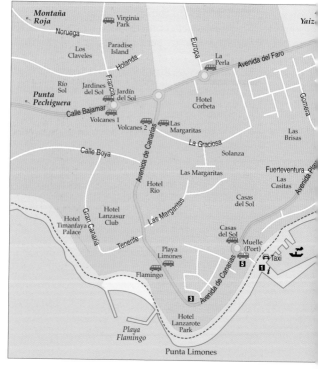

ARRECIFE

1   Tourist information
2   Bus station
3   Police
4   Hospital
5   Archaeological museum
    (Castillo de San Gabriel)
6   Art gallery (Castillo de San José)
7   Town hall
8   Fish market
9   Post office
10 Clinics
11 Casa de Cultura
12 Cabildo building and
    Intercambiador (main bus stop)
13 Shopping centres

City exits

A   → airport and
        Puerto del Carmen
B   → San Bartolomé and Tinajo
C   → Teguise
D   → port and Costa Teguise

ARRECIFE

PLAYA BLANCA

1   Tourist information; also ferry ticket
    offices (ferries to Corralejo,
    Puerto del Carmen, Lobos)
2   Post office
3   Clinics
4   Waterside promenade with shops
    and restaurants
5   Shopping centres
6   Bus station (🚌 intercity bus;
    🚐 town bus 30 with name of stop)

PLAYA BLANCA

Playa Blanca town bus

A town bus, Line 30, plies a circuit within Playa Blanca, calling at the most popular parts of the resort. Stops include Las Coloradas and the Rubicón Marina (Alternative walk 18 and Walk 20), the port (boats to Lobos and Fuerteventura), Virginia Park (Walk 21) and Faro Park (Walk 28). Buses depart the station daily 06.30-22.00, every 30 minutes on the hour and the half-hour.

🌼 Picnicking

Picnicking isn't one of Lanzarote's strong points. Shade is the biggest problem — there are not many trees on the island! Nor are there any 'organised' picnic sites, as there are on other Canary Islands — unless you count the few tables at El Bosquecillo.

Nevertheless, there *are* many lovely picnic spots — if you know where to look. Throughout the car tours I call your attention to both *roadside* picnic spots (most of them in shade) and the more remote settings you can reach during a fairly short walk. On the following pages I tell you more about these off-the-beaten-track locations, which I've come upon when out walking. Note that picnic numbers correspond to walk numbers, so you can quickly find the general location on the island by referring to the pull-out touring map (where the walks are highlighted in green). Most of the spots I've chosen are very easy to reach, and I outline transport details (🚐: bus information; 🚗: where to park for motorists), walking times, and views or setting. Beside the picnic title, you'll also find a map reference: the *precise* location of the picnic spot is shown on the relevant large-scale *walking* map by the

symbol *P*. Some of the picnic settings are also illustrated; if so, a photograph reference follows the map reference.

If you have just one day for picnicking, don't miss Picnic 2 (Risco de Famara). I think this is one of the loveliest and most memorable places to enjoy a picnic in the entire archipelago.

Please glance over the comments before you start off on your picnic: if some walking is involved, remember to wear sensible shoes and to take a sunhat (○ = picnic in full sun). It's a good idea to take along a plastic sheet as well, in case the ground is damp or prickly.

If you are travelling to your picnic by bus, be sure to verify departure times in advance. Although there are timetables in this book, they do change from time to time, without prior warning. **If you are travelling to your picnic by car**, *never* block a road or track when you park.

All picnickers should read the country code on page 18 and go quietly in the countryside. *Buen provecho!*

Picnic suggestions

1 LA GRACIOSA (map page 43) ○

by ⚓: 20-25min on foot. Ferry from Orzola to La Graciosa
Off the ferry, skirt the waterfront, heading west, and continue around in front of and through the houses on the shore. Beyond the houses you come to a superb beach and shortly after, a tidal lagoon. It's a fantastic spot, from where you look across to the Risco de Famara.

2 RISCO DE FAMARA (map pages 46-47, photograph page 12) ○

by 🚗 only: 5-10min on foot. Park southwest of the Mirador del Río: descending from the *mirador* as in Car tour 1, watch for two derelict stone buildings just below the road on the right, 2.3km from the *mirador*. Just past them and just before the large Finca La Corona on the left, turn right on a narrow stone-paved track. Follow this track 100m to a small car park. Coming from the south, the track is on the left, just past the Finca La Corona.
Sit on the ledge of the cliff, below the track, and overlook the Mirador del Río vista — now you'll have the view almost all to yourself. No other picnic spot on the island matches this one. Cliffs provide the only shade.

El Golfo is a fine spot for a picnic. While there are many tourists coming and going, they don't stay very long — and some don't even explore as far as this cloudy green lagoon, the Charco de los Clicos. The crater walls provide ample shade.

4 MAGUEZ (map pages 46-47, photograph pages 52-53) ○

by 🚌: 40min on foot. Bus to Máguez and follow Walk 4.

by 🚗: 25min on foot. On entering Máguez *from the north*, you encounter a fork in the road: bear left and, a few hundred metres/yards along, you will see a track cutting back sharply to the left. Park at the side of the road here, without obstructing traffic. Entering Máguez *from the south*, use the map to drive along the walking route and park as above

Set off along the track and picnic anywhere you like. My favourite spot is just beyond the intersection at the 35min-point (page 51). Here you can picnic on a grassy hillock, with a lovely view over cultivated slopes down to the east coast, and Monte Corona standing just behind you.

View from the Mirador del Río down over the salt pans shown on page 45 and across to La Graciosa (Picnic 2 offers similar views).

Cultivation at the foot of the path below the mirador *at Haría (Picnic 7a)*

6 LOS HELECHOS (map pages 46-47, photograph page 56) ○

by 🚙 only: 5-35min on foot. Park below Los Helechos (see the notes for Short walk 6 on page 56).

There are many places to picnic on grassy slopes — at the edge of the plateau (5min), by the white building (10min), from where you look down to a farm and the Risco cliffs and La Graciosa, or at the trig point (35min). Some shade at the white building.

7a OVERLOOKING HARIA (map page 64, nearby photographs pages 62-63 and above) ○

by 🚌 and 🚕 taxi: 1h on foot. Do Short walk 7-1 (page 60).

by 🚗: 10-20min on foot. Park at the Restaurante Los Helechos (with *mirador*) on the LZ10 above Haría. Follow Short walk 7-1 (page 60) for as long as you like.

The setting is a flower-filled old pilgrims' trail, from where you have wonderful views down the Valle de Malpaso and over Haría.

7b VALLE DE LOS CASTILLEJOS (map page 64, photograph page 18) ○

by 🚌 or 🚗 to Haría: 20min on foot.

Follow Short walk 7-2 (page 60) for as long as you like; there are lovely views over cultivation and to Máguez after about 10min.

9 ERMITA DE LAS NIEVES (map pages 68-69, photographs pages 64 and 72) ○

by 🚗 only: up to 5min on foot. Park by the Ermita de las Nieves, off the LZ10.

Picnic anywhere on the top of the crest. The views across the centre of Lanzarote and out to its neighbouring islands are magnificent (but take great care by the cliffs, especially on windy days). There is some shade from the chapel walls.

10 ERMITA DE SAN JOSE (map pages 68-69) ○

by 🚗: no walking. Park by the chapel ruins, off the LZ10 outside Teguise. These large honey-coloured ruins are opposite the Castillo de Santa Bárbara and are easily seen from the road. Use the large-scale map on pages 68-69 to drive there.

These old ruins are picturesque and provide some shade. They are passed near the end of Walk 9 and at the beginning of Walk 10.

11 PEÑA DE LA PEQUEÑA (map pages 68-69, photograph page 75) ○

by 🚗: 10-25min on foot. Drive to the track off the LZ10, 100m south of the km22 road marker (see page 75, last paragraph, to drive along the walking route; park near the start of the track, opposite a small house). *Follow the track, overlooking the Paloma Valley on the right and the Chafariz/Cuchillo Valley on the left, as far as you like.*

13 LA CALDERETA (map page 81, photographs pages 80-81) ○

by 🚐 (about 1h) or 🚗: about 40min on foot: see Walk 13 on page 80. *Follow the walk to the Caldereta and picnic at the refugio (ample places to sit). Wear boots or very sturdy shoes! Overlook the greenery of this small crater.*

Playa de Papagayo (Picnic 20). If you enjoy some sand in your sarnies, then this is the most beautiful setting on the island for a picnic on the beach.

14 MONTAÑA DE GUARDILAMA (map pages 84-85, photograph page 86) ○

by 🚐: 1h on foot. Bus to Uga and follow Walk 14 on page 82.
by 🚗: 10-45min on foot. Turn off the LZ30 (La Geria road) 600m/yds past the junction north of Uga (just past the km22 stone), onto the first track forking off east (with several walkers' and bikers' fingerposts). Park off the side of the road; don't block the track (up to 45min on foot).
Follow the track to the pass below Guardilama (45min), or go only as far as you wish up the track. You have a superb view over the dark Geria Valley — quite a sight when the vines are coming into leaf (photographs pages 28-29 and 82).

17 ATALAYA DE FEMES (map page 91, photos pages 89, 101) ○

by 🚗: up to 1h on foot (bus times are inconvenient for short walks). Park in Femés and follow Short walk 17 on page 89.
Picnic above the first crater (from where your views will be limited), or carry on to the summit another 25 minutes further up. From there you will have an excellent view of the volcanoes of Timanfaya and the south of the island — as well as the northern part of Fuerteventura. Note that this is a strenuous climb, and it can be very windy and cool!

18 DEGOLLADA DEL PORTUGUES (map pages 94-95, photograph page 102) ○

by 🚗: about 50min on foot (bus times are inconvenient for short walks). Park in Femés.
Follow Short walk 18 on page 93 to just over the 45min-point.
A very isolated setting overlooking the Barranco de los Dises, across to Hacha Grande.

20 PLAYA DE PAPAGAYO (map pages 94-95, photograph opposite) ○

by 🚗 only: 5min-1h on foot. From the roundabout by the petrol station at Playa Blanca follow the notes on pages 33-34 (5min on foot). The track is very bumpy; you may prefer to park as suggested in Shorter walk 20 on page 102 (1h on foot).
Expect company here: Playa de Papagayo is highlighted in all the guides. There are good spots in the cove or on the rocky promontory to the right of the beach. Punta de Papagayo, less than 10 minutes away, is usually quiet, but usually windy too! Caleta del Congrio (an unofficial naturist beach) and the other beaches lining the coast also make splendid picnic spots.

21 MONTAÑA ROJA (map page 107, photo pages 106-107) ○

by 🚗 only: 40min on foot. Follow Walk 21, page 106.
Fine views over the Punta de Pechiguera and to Fuerteventura.

22 JANUBIO (map pages 110-111, photos pages 109, 110) ○

by 🚐: 1h or more on foot. Bus to La Hoya; follow Walk 22, page 108.
by 🚗: 10-15min on foot. Park at the water desalination building off the LZ701 road, some 2.4km south of the El Golfo roundabout.
Find a choice spot amidst the rocks fringing the shore. The beautiful rock pools lie about 10-15min southwest of the desalination plant.

❋ Touring

Hiring a vehicle is good value on Lanzarote, and there are car rental offices in abundance in all the tourist centres — but you are still likely to get a better price if you book before you travel. And you won't use a lot of petrol driving these relatively short distances, so all in all, car hire will be good value.

Drive carefully! Excess speed on some of the very straight roads is probably the main reason why *Lanzarote has the highest level of traffic accidents in all Spain.*

But as a tourist, your chief problem may be the many roundabouts built since the death of César Manrique. Manrique had argued for years that the Tahiche intersection on the main Arrecife/Teguise road was dangerous, and that visitors to his foundation might be injured. In 1992 he was himself killed in a crash at this very spot. Since his death, roundabouts have been built all over the island. Unfortunately, while many of them are, literally, works of art, some are extremely complicated and especially challenging for the newly-arrived visitor. Remember that — *of course* — traffic already on the roundabout has priority.

Another hazard may be the deep unprotected drop at the side of some newly-surfaced roads — not always obvious when you screech to a halt and pull over at an 'unofficial' viewpoint, but you risk losing your transmission!

The touring notes are brief: they contain little history or information readily available in free tourist office leaflets or standard

Isolated farm near Timanfaya

guides. The main tourist centres and towns are not described either, for the same reason. Instead, I concentrate on the 'logistics' of touring: times and distances, road conditions, and seeing places many tourists miss. Most of all I emphasise possibilities for **walking** and **picnicking**. While some of the references to picnics off the beaten track may not be suitable during a long car tour, you may see a landscape that you would like to explore at leisure another day, when you've more time to stretch your legs.

The large fold-out touring map is designed to be held out opposite the touring notes and contains all the information you will need outside the towns. The tours have been written up starting from Puerto del Carmen, but I also suggest where best to join them if you are based at Playa Blanca or Costa Teguise. Town plans with exits for motorists are on pages 6-9. Remember to allow plenty of time for visits, and to take along warm clothing as well as some food and drink, in case you are delayed. The distances quoted in the notes are cumulative from Puerto del Carmen. A key to **symbols** used in the touring notes is on the touring map.

All motorists should read the country code on page 18 and go quietly in the countryside. *Buen viaje!*

A country code for walkers and motorists

The experienced rambler is used to following a 'country code', but the tourist out for a lark may unwittingly cause damage, harm animals, and even endanger his own life. Please heed this advice.

- **Do not light fires.**
- **Do not frighten animals.** The goats and sheep you may encounter on your walks are not tame.
- **Walk quietly** through all hamlets and villages.
- **Leave all gates just as you find them.** Although you may not see any animals, the gates do have a purpose — generally to keep goats or sheep in (or out of) an area.
- **Protect all wild and cultivated plants.** Don't try to pick wild flowers or uproot saplings. Obviously fruit and other crops are someone's private property and should not be touched. Never walk over cultivated land.
- **Take all your litter away with you.**
- **Walkers — *Do not take risks!*** This is the most important point of all. Do not attempt walks beyond your capacity, and do not wander off the paths described here if there is any sign of mist or if it is late in the day. Do *not* walk alone, and *always* tell a responsible person exactly where you are going and what time you plan to return. Remember, if you become lost or injure yourself, it may be a long time before you are found. On any but a very short walk close to villages, be sure to take a torch, whistle, extra water and warm clothing — as well as some high-energy food, like chocolate. Read and re-read the important note on page 2, as well as the guidelines on grade and equipment for each walk you plan to do!

Haría's Valle de los Castillejos (Picnic 7b), with Máguez and Monte Corona in the background

Car tour 1: THE SIGHTS OF THE NORTH

Puerto del Carmen • Tahiche • Arrieta • Jameos del Agua • Cueva de los Verdes • Orzola • Mirador del Río • Haría • Teguise • La Caleta de Famara • Mozaga • Puerto del Carmen

143km/89mi; about 3h30min driving; Exit A from Puerto del Carmen

On route: roadside picnics at a chapel near Orzola, Haría, or at El Bosquecillo (⌂); also Picnics 2, 4, 6, 7a, 7b, 9, 10 (see pages 10-14 and *P* symbol in the text); Walks 2-10, (11), 14, 16, 19, (23, 26), 25, 27, 30

Although the driving time is only three and one-half hours, allow an entire day for this tour if you want to visit all the tourist attractions. Roads are generally good, but often narrow. Cloud and mist are not infrequent in the northern hills, and visibility can be reduced to almost zero! Look out for livestock on the roads and for pedestrians in the villages. A low speed is recommended for these roads. Arrecife is not included in this tour because it is well served by public transport and may be visited another day.

From Costa Teguise take the Guatiza road (LZ34) and join the tour on the LZ1 after passing through the arch with the cross. From Playa Blanca take the LZ2 and join the tour as you pass above the airport.

Opening hours
Cactus Garden, Guatiza: 10.00-17.45 daily
Jameos del Agua: 10.00-18.30 daily; also 19.00-02.00 (Tue/Fri/Sat)
Cueva de los Verdes: 10.00-18.00 daily
Mirador del Río: 10.00-17.45 daily
Museo de Arte Sacro de Haría: 11.00-13.00 daily
Guinate Tropical Park: 10.00-17.00 daily
Castillo de Santa Bárbara, Teguise (Museo del Emigrante Canario):
   Summer: 10.00-15.00 (Mon-Fri), 10.00-14.00 (Sat/Sun); *Winter:*
   10.00-16.00 (Mon-Fri), 10.00-15/00 (Sat/Sun)
Palacio Spinola, Teguise: 09.00-15.00 (Mon, Tue, Thu, Fri); 09.30-13.30 (Sat/Sun); closed Wednesdays
Teguise market: 09.00-14.00 (Sun)
Museo Agrícola, Tiagua: 10.00-17.00 (Mon-Fri); 10.00-14.30 (Sat)

Apart from the Timanfaya National Park and the Geria Valley, the northern part of Lanzarote is the most scenically interesting. As you follow this tour, winding your way around and over the northern massif, you'll encounter the extraordinarily beautiful colours, shapes and textures that create the landscape canvas of Lanzarote. The Cueva de los Verdes — a vast volcanic tube measuring one kilometre in length, may be the most intriguing cave you've ever seen. You'll also learn who César Manrique was and what he meant to the island — or, rather, what his native land meant to him.

Leave Puerto del Carmen (Walks 14, 16, 19, 27) by heading east on the Avenida de las Playas (Exit A). Follow 'Arrecife, Yaiza'. As you pass a sign denoting the end of Puerto del Carmen, Canary date palms line both sides of the road and you are heading towards Montaña Blanca on the left and Montaña Mina on the right — with the

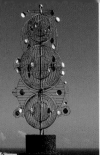

Some roundabouts are works of art. These 'wind sculptures' are both by César Manrique (left: just south of Tahiche; right: Arrieta).

wind generators that were a 'pilot project' for the larger installation seen later in the tour. As you approach a roundabout/flyover, keep right for Arrecife. This takes you onto the LZ2 (7km), and you drive above the airport. Be sure to get into the left-hand lane for 'Circunvalación', and at the first major junction go off left for 'Circunvalación' and 'Costa Teguise', joining the LZ3 (Arrecife ring road). At the next major junction (where San Bartolomé is to the left), go straight over for 'Pto. Marmoles' and 'Costa Teguise'. There were roadworks here when we checked, and the next, third junction has been badly signposted for years in any case. ***You want 'Tahiche' (easily missed), not Arrecife, not Marmoles, not Costa Teguise!***

After 2km you should come upon the 'whirling whisks' roundabout shown above left, where you go straight over for 'Tahiche'. (A left turn here leads to the Fundación Manrique, and it was at this junction that César Manrique was killed in 1992.) Just inside **Tahiche** (20km ✕) turn right for 'Orzola, Jameos del Agua', joining the LZ1 and passing through an open flat countryside pierced by prominent isolated hills. Pass the road to Costa Teguise (Walks 23, 26); from here its gateway, with a cross on top, looks like a chapel. At 27km turn right past gardens squared off by stone walls to the Moorish-flavoured village of **Guatiza** (29km). The village itself is swallowed up amidst fields of prickly pear. Leaving the village, pass the cactus garden (**Jardín de Cactus★**) on your right; a well-preserved windmill stands above it.

Soon the entire plain is taken over by prickly pear. Farmed prickly pear is an unusual sight — normally we see it growing wild. The cochineal insect is bred on these plants: the female lives off the juice of the cactus leaf (see photograph page 67), and after three months is harvested and dried in the sun. Today cochineal is used as colouring in lipsticks, toothpastes, and some drinks — Campari and Martini, for instance. The dye was once important in the carpet industry and during the 1800s was a major money-earner for Lanzarote. Off the sea-plain you look up into

The Torrecilla del Domingo, backed by the jagged rim of Monte Corona. Both are landmarks on any visit to the north of the island. Walk 4 circles them; Walk 5 climbs up to the crater's rim.

ridges that trail off the northern hills. **Mala** (32km ✕; Walk 9), another spacious farming village, follows. The 'Lanzarote colours' can be seen in the white façades and green doorways and window shutters of the houses. Some 3km outside the village you pass the LZ207 road up left to Tabayesco, where Walk 11 begins and ends.*

In need of eggs, saucepans, or perhaps sunglasses? Then just pull into the petrol station with supermarket and café in **Arrieta** (37km ⛽✕🛏), a small seaside village built along the rocky shore. At the roundabout just past here, the revolving red cones shown opposite are another of Manrique's confections. Follow 'Orzola', then bear right almost immediately for Jameos del Agua, ignoring the road left to the Mirador del Río. Pass **Punta Mujeres** (38km ✕), a tight cluster of dwellings. A few minutes later branch off right for **Jameos del Agua★** (42km ✕M), one of the island's most popular tourist attractions. This enchanting cave is the result of two opposing forces — man and nature. A splendid compromise has been reached: the eruption of Monte Corona was responsible for the natural element; César Manrique was the man. The cave has been skillfully transformed into a bar/restaurant and night club, maintaining as much natural décor as possible. Penetrating into the depths of the cave, you come to a large crystal-clear sea-pool. Shiny objects on the floor of the pool catch your eye: tiny white blind crabs (*Munidopsis polymorpha*), unique in the sea world. You then ascend to the swimming pool shown overleaf, set in a colourful rock garden. Before you leave, be sure to visit the 'Casa de los Volcanes' incorporated in the complex, a museum devoted to volcanism throughout the world.

Return to the main road, cross it, and head up to the **Cueva de los Verdes★**, 0.5km away. Only one of the

---

*Sometime during your visit, make a circuit of the beautiful Chafariz Valley (Walk 11; photograph page 75): turn up this road (🚗) and, when you come into Haría, turn right for 'Arrieta'. Descending the far side of the valley, you rejoin the main road by the 'red cones' roundabout shown opposite (above).

21

Jameos del Agua

seven kilometres of this vast complex of tunnels is open to the public. With a guide, you wind down through low, narrow passageways and emerge into enormous cool chambers — one of them an auditorium with perfect acoustics. The Guanches sought refuge in these caves whenever there were pirate raids. The caves were created when streams of molten lava from Monte Corona flowed beneath a hardened outside crust (see pages 119-120).

Back on the main road, turn left for Orzola. Following the coast, you run along the edge of the Malpais ('Badlands') de la Corona — an expansive undulating plateau of lava carpeted in a thick mat of greenery. Monte Corona — a massive sharp-rimmed crater that dominates the north of the island — broods lonely and impressive on the left. Patches of sand and a couple of sandy coves embraced in the rocky shoreline break up the lava flow (photograph page 123). Soon the table-topped island of Alegranza appears over to your right — and the north of La Graciosa. Rocky reefs create lagoons along the shoreline, and these are ideal for swimming.

The Famara massif rises up into a bold block of hills behind **Orzola** (53km ⌂✕ and ⛴ to La Graciosa) and its port. Here's where you catch the ferry, if you're planning to do Walk 1 or picnic on La Graciosa. There's also a pleasant coastal walk to Punta Fariones (Walk 25).

Now making for the Mirador del Río, climb inland, after 500m passing a chapel on the left, a pleasant picnic spot with some shade. Still circling the *malpais* on a narrow winding road (LZ203), a wavy blanket of greenery, pierced by rocky outcrops, stretches below. Join the LZ201 at the foot of Monte Corona and ascend to the right. Thick stone walls soon take over the country-side; their precision transforms the fields into a work of art. An imposing solitary villa, the Torrecilla del Domingo, rises up out of this maze of walls, crowning a hilltop. You pass above the Quemada crater; Walk 4 circles it. Walk 5, which ascends Monte Corona, could begin at the church in Ye, a small farming community cast across a sloping plateau below Corona's gaping crater. But for this tour, turn right on the outskirts of the village for 'Mirador del Río'. Crossing the plateau, you look straight down into deep valleys. In spring the top of the plateau is flecked with poppies, daisies and *Echium*.

A porthole window set in a stone wall enclosing the car park is all that gives away the **Mirador del Río★** (📷; paid admission), built on the site of a 16th-century watch-tower. This well-camouflaged viewpoint is embedded in the top of the **Risco (Cliff) de Famara★**. From here you look straight out over the Río channel onto the bare and barren — yet strangely beautiful — Graciosa Island, which sits just below (photographs pages 41 and 48). This is a view unequalled on Lanzarote, and one of the best vistas in all the Canaries. The mountain island (Montaña Clara) and Alegranza enhance this already-magnificent sea view. The *mirador* balcony hangs out over a precipitous wall plummeting 450m/1475ft below ... down to the landscapes of Walk 2 — the exquisite Playa del Risco and the captivating salt pans of El Río. Note: the exterior of this setting is worth seeing from the cliff-top above the *mirador* (from where the photographs on pages 13 and 48 were taken).

From the *mirador* fork right, to continue south along the edge of the Famara cliffs (LZ202). This wall of rock stretches for 23km and reaches a height of 600m/1970ft, as it slices its way along the northwest coast. The road is narrow, but built up at the sides; priority is given to traffic travelling in this direction. You recapture the very dramatic *mirador* vista a little further on, where you are able to pull over safely. In the distance ahead you see the vast Jable plain stretching inland behind the Playa de Famara, and the hills growing up out of the west coast.

Leaving the plateau you overlook a rocky basin of farmland on the far side of Ye. Some 2.4km from the *mirador* you pass the stone-laid track to the most stunning picnic spot on the island (*P2*). After another 200m, just below Monte Corona, come to a stop sign at a T-junction and turn right for Haría. Pass the turn-off to the Guinate

Tropical Park, where the circuit of Los Helechos (*P*6 and Walk 6) ends — by car or on foot. When you come to a Y-fork, keep right for 'Arrecife' (but to park for *P*4, in the setting shown on page 57, go left.)

Máguez (72km ✕) is a rambling, pleasantly scruffy country village with a peaceful air about it. Walk 6 circles the very quiet and scenic mound of volcanoes up to the right. Keep straight on through the village, and take care at the stop sign in the centre, where buildings totally obscure your view of crossing traffic.

Over in the next valley lies **Haría** (74km ✕*MP*7b), the handsome settlement shown on pages 1, 13, 18, and 62-63. This oasis of greenery boasts the largest number of palms in the Canaries. (I wonder what La Gomera has to say about this?) Bougainvillea, geraniums, and hibiscus splash the village with colour, and the lovely shady plaza adds a touch of class. Keep right on coming into the village and then right again into the one-way system. Turn left at the crossroads (where the road ahead is marked as no entry), pass the town hall on the right, and then go right at the T-junction for 'Arrecife por Teguise'. As you leave Haría, you could picnic in good shade just past the Cortijo restaurant on the right (ample parking, a wall to sit on).

Exiting this valley of palms you wind up a rocky crest in tight hairpins. Some 4km uphill, there are fine views from the white 'Mirador de Haría' building (⌦). Then, 1km further on, there's another superb outlook from the Restaurante Los Helechos (79km ⌦✕*P*7a), where Walk 7 starts. Some 200m past here, ignore a road off right sign-posted 'Mirador Riscos de Famara' (climbed in Walk 8).* Pass a roadside *mirador* and, 650m further on, the track to Picnic 11 (at the end of a row of palms). You're now below Lanzarote's highest point, the **Peñas del Chache** (670m/2200ft; photograph page 64), which houses a military installation. Save for the 'golf ball' radar installa-tion on top, you'd hardly notice it. What *does* catch the eye are the wind generators of the Parque Eólico ahead.

Just under 3km from the Helechos restaurant, turn right towards 'Las Nieves'. This recently rebuilt chapel (*P*9; photographs on pages 64 and 72) stands in solitude, high on a windswept plateau, marking the site where the Virgin appeared to a young shepherd. The chapel is open

---

*The second turning right off this road leads to a splendid picnic spot in Lanzarote's only 'forest', El Bosquecillo ('the Little Wood'; ⌦ ⌁). This shaded viewpoint atop the Famara cliffs, with a few tables, is very popular with the locals at weekends.

on Saturdays between 14.30 and 18.00 and on the 5th of August, the patron saint's day. From the edge of the plateau you have a splendid view down onto the extensive Playa de Famara and over the semi-desert Jable plain. The Risco de Famara topples off to an abrupt end here.

Head back to the main road, passing the entrance to the **Parque Eólico**. Stone walls fence off the countryside on your approach to Los Valles. The interior of the island

Church at Teguise; see also photograph pages 70-71.

opens up, as low-slung valleys peel back and rounded hillocks rise in the background. Serried ranks of American aloes line the road as it descends in curves (✷). **Los Valles** (88km; Walk 10) sits on the edge of a sweeping basin patched in huge cultivated squares. Here you find the best examples of traditional Arcadian houses — low oblong buildings with very few (and very small) windows. Haystacks set amidst the houses and farm buildings set off this rural landscape.

Beyond Los Valles you cross the basin as you head towards Teguise. Rising ahead on the left is the 16th-century Castillo de Santa Bárbara (■M). This modest fortress commands a good view over the surrounding countryside from its perch at the edge of the Guanapay crater. Once a watchtower to warn against the raiding Moors, it now appropriately houses a small piracy museum. Below, to the right, you will see some substantial honey-hued ruins — the old Ermita de San José (*P*10).

Walks 8-10 visit **Teguise★** (95km ✷✝M and Sunday market), the island's ancient capital … and Lanzarote's showplace. This exquisite village still retains its original character of cobbled streets, stately old buildings, and spacious plazas. In the main square you'll find the imposing main church, Nuestra Señora de Guadalupe, facing the 18th-century Palacio Spinola. The Tourist Office is here, too. Pick up a town plan and plan to spend a couple of hours exploring the various welcoming plazas, as well as the Santo Domingo and San Francisco convents.

Leaving the glaring whiteness of Teguise, follow signs for Mozaga and the Monumento al Campesino, to get on the LZ30 (🚌). Some 3km along, turn right for 'La Caleta' (LZ402). The fishing village of **La Caleta de Famara** (112km ▲✷) boasts some fine seafood restaurants. To reach the quieter end of this long sandy beach, drive through the **Famara** *urbanización* and follow the rough track below the cliffs. Walk 3 explores this area.

From La Caleta make for Tiagua on the LZ401. Beyond **Sóo** and **Munique** you pass the Villa Agrícola, a museum of countryside life, before coming into **Tiagua** (✷M). Turn left on the LZ20 towards 'Arrecife'. At **Mozaga** (✷🚌) you come to a roundabout at the Monu-mento al Campesino★ (see Car tour 2 and photograph on page 31) and go straight over to **San Bartolomé** (✷M). From here keep straight through on the LZ20 to the Arrecife ring road, then retrace your outgoing route, coming back into **Puerto del Carmen** after 143km.

Car tour 2: TIMANFAYA AND THE SOUTHERN BEACHES

Puerto del Carmen • San Bartolomé • Tinajo • La Santa • Montañas del Fuego • Yaiza • El Golfo • Playa Blanca • Playa de Papagayo • Femés • La Geria Valley • San Bartolomé • Puerto del Carmen

150km/93mi; 4 hours driving (plus 1 hour's coach tour in the national park); Exit B from Puerto del Carmen

On route: roadside picnics at La Isleta, El Golfo, Femés; also Picnics 14-22 (see pages 10-14 and *P* symbol in the text); Walks 12-22, 24, 27-30

Roads are good with only one exception at present: the rough track to Papagayo (about 6km each way; toll payable) is only recommended for beach enthusiasts; it's very bumpy and also on the route of jeep safaris — you'll taste a lot of dust when they pass. (The once-narrow road in the Geria valley has recently been widened and should pose no problems.) Between Yaiza and Playa Blanca this tour follows the old road (LZ701); the newer LZ2 is the 'fast track'.

From Costa Teguise *take the Arrecife ring road and join the tour at San Bartolomé (the 11km-point).* ***From Playa Blanca*** *begin at the roundabout by the petrol station: take the 'old road' (LZ701) signposted to Yaiza and, at the junction for El Golfo, turn off for Las Breñas, joining the tour on page 34 (last paragraph) and finishing the circuit when you return to Playa Blanca.*

Opening hours

Timanfaya National Park: 09.00-17.45 daily, with coach tours from 10.00-17.00 daily, every half hour (included in the entry fee)
Timanfaya Visitors' Centre, Mancha Blanca: 09.00-17.00 daily
Monumento al Campesino (house and museum): 10.00-18.00 daily; restaurant 12.00-16.30 daily
Museo del Vino (Masdache): 10.30-18.00 daily (free entrance)
Museo Etnográfico Tanit, San Bartolomé: 10.00-14.00 Mon-Sat

T his southern route allows you plenty of time for short strolls, a swim, and perhaps some wine-tasting — if you make a day of it. Vulcanology may not be one of your favourite topics, but this drive will certainly arouse your interest. Violent eruptions in the 18th and 19th centuries have left a curious landscape in their wake. The national park bus tour — a must for everyone — immerses you in this moonscape of rich volcanic hues. It will be the highlight of your day, if not of your entire holiday on Lanzarote. More curiosities follow, however. La Geria, the valley of ash, and the home of *malvasía* wine, is another amazing sight. Here the vineyards create a scenery of their own. The eroded Golfo crater, with its dazzling green lagoon, is something akin to an artist's palette, with all its colours and blended hues. And if all this isn't enough, then there are the golden sandy beaches of the southeast, of which Papagayo has become the most popular amongst tourists. You'll soon see why.

Leave Puerto del Carmen on the Tías road (Exit B). Follow signs for Tías at first. Just before Tías, at a roundabout, turn right for Arrecife. Then follow signs for San Bartolomé. You bypass Tías and wind up over hills on the LZ35, into a vast sloping valley, with Montaña Blanca to the left and Montaña Mina ahead to the right, crowned with wind generators. Vivid splashes of scarlet poppies, white daisies, and yellow dandelions light up the surrounding farmlands in spring. Head straight through the sprawling village of **San Bartolomé** (11km ✗M), following signs for Teguise, and, when you meet the LZ20, turn left for Tinajo.

At a roundabout (14km ✗⌶) you're confronted with another of Manrique's works — the **Monumento al Campesino**★, dedicated to the island's country dwellers. This bold structure, shown overleaf, stands in pleasant surroundings, with a restaurant (a beautifully-restored farmhouse) that specialises in local dishes, a souvenir shop, and a small 'farmyard' of great appeal to children. On the far side of the roundabout, you come into the hamlet of **Mozaga**. The setting is very picturesque: the houses are dispersed amidst great blocks of lava, which are brightly speckled with green *Aeoniums*. Neat, fresh-green garden plots border the lava plain.

Tao (17km ✗⌨) occupies a slight rise with a fine view across the sweeping Jable plain to the cliffs of Famara and the islands. A sprinkling of elegant palms complements this pleasant rural setting. You pass through **Tiagua** (18km ✗M) in the thick of these gardens.

An well-landscaped avenue of cacti and palms leads you into the expansive farming settlement of **Tinajo** (23km

✕➤), where Walk 12 ends. Entering the village, turn right for La Santa at the roundabout. Descending to the coast, red Montaña Bermeja catches your eye, rising off the shore below to the left. The countryside becomes harsher, rough and bumpy with hillocks, and the terrain is strewn with stones. **La Santa** (✕) is a small village of restaurants set back off the shore. Continue to Club La Santa, a rather exclusive sports complex 2km further on (30km ▲▲ ✕). It overlooks the rocky islet, La Isleta, and a pretty lagoon — a pleasant interlude in this desolate stretch of coast. To cross to the *isleta*, curve left past the hotel reception and when you come to a roundabout, keep right. Circle halfway round the islet; then, keeping the lagoon just to your left, cross the causeway and return to the main road. Opposite is a large parking area under palms; you can picnic here on lava jetties near the sea or by the lagoon.

Returning to Tinajo, keep straight on through the village for 'Mancha Blanca', soon enjoying a pretty view left to the small village of La Vegueta. Just as you enter **Mancha Blanca** (41km; starting point for Walks 12 and 13), turn right for 'P N Timanfaya'. Mancha Blanca rests on a shelf overlooking its tidy ash fields, on the edge of a sea of lava that floods the southwest. Everything here grows in straight rows. The village is the home of the island's female patron saint — Our Lady of the Volcanoes, who is credited with having saved Tinajo from a lava flow.

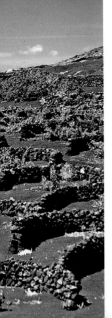

A popular festival celebrates the saint's day on September 15th.

At 42km the road bends left and a track straight ahead leads to parking for the ascent of Montaña Blanca (Walk 13), from where you would look into the gaping crater shown on page 4. At 43.5km you enter the national park; the Visitors' Centre is 100m along on the right. Even if you're not going to book for Walk 24, *do* stop here to see the audiovisual show and study the exhibits, to better appreciate the landscape ahead! Once beyond the Visitors' Centre you mount the lava plateau,

Vineyards in La Geria lead the eye to the Fire Mountains of Timanfaya

The Monumento al Campesino is a pleasant place to take a break

and another world awaits you: the world of fire and brimstone, where just under 300 years ago all hell let loose. As Yaiza's parish priest described it: 'the earth suddenly opened up and an enormous mountain rose from the bosom of the earth and from its apex shot flames which continued to burn for 19 days'. This catastrophic eruption lasted intermittently for some six years (1730 to 1736), burying one-third of the island (including eleven villages and many more hamlets) under metres of lava ... an eruption unsurpassed in recorded history. Less than one hundred years later another eruption increased the existing number of new volcanoes in the area from 26 to 29.

Crossing this lonely but curiously beautiful landscape (photographs pages 16-17 and 116-121) is like being on another planet, hence it should come as no surprise to learn that the first astronauts were shown photographs of the national park in preparation for their moon flight. The road cuts its way through rough, sharp 'AA' lava. Lichen flecks the rock, creating the impression of freshly fallen sleet. Pale pink wild geraniums stand out poignantly in this black world. Their leaves are dried by the locals and made into tea — a good source of vitamin C. Assorted volcanoes, with hints of red, clay brown, and deep maroon, grow out of the lava.

Large mounds of cinder soon close in on you. Some 9km from Mancha Blanca, at a mini-roundabout, turn off right for the **Islote de Hilario** — departure point for the coach tours around the **Montañas del Fuego★**. An entrance fee, which includes the tour, is paid here. The *islote* is named for the hermit Hilario, who returned here after the eruptions had subsided to build a hut and plant a fig tree (which, incidentally, is *not* the fig in the restaurant). The restaurant here makes good use of thermal energy —

the temperature reaches 360°C only six metres below the surface of the ground. Your excursion bus twists up, down, and around the great volcanoes, affording stunning views over the park and into the craters, which drip with endless blends of colours.

Leaving the Islote de Hilario and continuing south, you pass alongside the russet-brown slopes of Pico Timanfaya (also called Pico del Fuego). Both the mountain and the park take their name from the village of Timanfaya, which thrived in this rich agricultural area before being destroyed by the eruptions. After 2km you pass the starting point for the much-publicised camel rides. You're bound to see a camel train ascending or descending — complete with awkwardly-seated tourists. It's an impressive sight, no matter how 'touristic'. Also, notice the lava formation on the left-hand side of the road here, with great cracks in its crust: this is *pahoehoe* lava (the name is Hawaiian; see photograph page 120).

Out of the lava fields come to a roundabout and cross the LZ2, to enter the charming white-washed village of **Yaiza** (61km ✗🛆⊕♟). Beyond the petrol station, turn right at the junction. You pass the cool, shady Los Remedios Square, with an 18th-century church of the same name. This proud village (see also photograph pages 90-91) has some fine old balconied houses, and the gardens overflow with colour. Walk 17 begins and ends here. On the outskirts of the village take the El Golfo exit from the roundabout. You enter more jagged lava fields; these are interrupted by *islotes* (islands of lava-free ground).

Meet the road to El Golfo (LZ704) and bear right. Bushes of resplendent green *tabaiba* light up the encompassing dark lava. Crossing a crest, a large *mirador* just before the village gives you an excellent view over the eroded Golfo craters. This majestic submarine volcano has been spectacularly eaten away by the sea, leaving one with the impression that it has been sliced in half. There's plenty of parking, and the more southerly access to the area has been closed, so if you want to walk down to the lagoon and crescent-shaped bay (*golfo*), do so now. Strolling down to the crater, you're greeted by a striking sight: an array of greys, browns, and reds oozes out of the cone and surrounding rock. A strong blue sea and a cloudy green lagoon (the **Charco de los Clicos**) ★ set at the base of the crater enhance this rainbow of colours (photographs pages 10-11 and 34). Although the area is fairly crowded, few people stay very long, and there are many

Shorter than Walk 29, this is a good leg-stretcher. From the Yaiza to El Golfo road, between the 4km and 5km markers, take the clear, motorable track going right (see map for Walk 29 on pages 118-119). Ignore two chained-off tracks going right into the national park and reach a junction 1.2km from the main road. Take the track straight ahead, between two tall white pillars. This track climbs and sweeps sharply right and then left as it runs to the left of two houses. It leads to a makeshift car park in a field, 100m below the lowest house. (Since the last bit of track is rough, it may be better to leave your car in the parking area just below the two houses.) Now follow the good (but no longer motorable) track into the national park and descend gradually. It is rough in places near the beginning, as rocks and lava have been deliberately strewn across it to deter jeeps, but then becomes a lovely stroll down between lava fields to Playa del Paso (30min). Note a path coming in across the lava fields from the right some 25 minutes along. This is the end of the coastal walk from Playa de la Madera (Walk 30). Playa del Paso is a beautiful, secluded black-sand beach.

pleasant picnic perches, with shade from the cliffs.

El Golfo★ (69km ✕🄿) is a cheerful seaside village of restaurants — the ideal base for Walk 29. Walk 30, the coastal hike from Playa de la Madera described on page 124, also ends here. Return to the junction for the village and head right for 'Playa Blanca' (LZ703). At a T-junction some 2km along, turn left (the right turn for access to the Charco de los Clicos has been permanently closed due to constant rockfall). Following the coastline further south, you drive through billowing waves of lava. Colourful Montaña Bermeja soon commands your attention with its glowing orange-brown cone. Just over 2km from El Golfo, turn right to a large parking area for **Los Hervideros**★ (🄿; the 'boiling springs'), where the sea pounds into sea-caves. Walkways have been carefully laid out through the maze of lava, where there are some impressive blow-holes when the sea is choppy. The sight is all the more impressive with the bright cone of Montaña Bermeja in the background (see photograph opposite). The lazy hills of Los Ajaches, leaning one against the other, rise up prominently ahead. Las Breñas is the village you see sprinkled along a raised shelf at the foot of the hills.

Turning inland, you round the **Salinas de Janubio**★ (🄿). They lie cradled in a deep basin off a land-locked lagoon and the curving black sand beach of Janubio. You look down onto a fine mosaic of tiny white squares of drying salt and ponds. The colours of this basin turn the severe countryside into quite a beauty spot, especially in the evening (see photograph page 112). Beyond the third viewpoint over the pans, you come to a roundabout at **La Hoya**: go right for 'Playa Blanca' on the LZ701. Some 600m along, a signposted *mirador* jutting out above the lagoon (⬚) enables you to view the *salinas* from the other side. This is the setting for Walk 22. Then, 1.8km from the view-point, you pass an isolated water desalination building (**P**22), from where you can also reach Walk 22.

Now crossing the featureless, stone-strewn Rubicón plain, you reach **Playa Blanca** (98km ⬚⬚⬚✕⬚ and ⬚ to Fuerteventura), once a small fishing village, but now the island's busiest resort. It's the focal point for several walks: the end of Alternative walk 18, the start of Walks 20 and 28, and the base for Walk 21. Moreover, Lobos (Walk 32) and Fuerteventura are enticingly close.

The road to Papagayo is signposted on the east side of the roundabout with the petrol station just outside Playa Blanca. At a T-junction turn right; then, at the next

Los Hervideros, with Montaña Bermeja in the background

Charco de los Clicos and the El Golfo crater — a fascinating example of marine erosion. See also pages 10-11.

crossing, turn left. Go over several crossroads until you come to a very large roundabout; turn right here on a track. After 2km, at a gatehouse, you must pay a toll. *Be warned:* this bumpy track is a jeep safari route. You might prefer to walk to Papagayo (see Shorter walk 20) — or even to take a cruise there another day (boats leave from the port at Playa Blanca). If you *do* decide to drive there, ignore tracks branching off in all directions to various beaches. Stay on the main track, just by following everyone else. You'll cross a barren stony shelf that lies at the foot of the Ajaches. All the beaches along here are different, and all are enticing. Before reaching Papagayo, branch off left to **Caleta del Congrio**, an unofficial (and, needless to say, very popular) naturist beach and **Puerto Muelas** (△). **Playa de Papagayo**, with two small bar/restaurants and spectacular beaches, is certainly worth the trip (*P*20; photograph page 14).

From Papagayo go back to the roundabout at the end of the dirt track and turn right for Femés on the LZ702. The road climbs to a pass below an antenna-topped hill, the Atalaya de Femés (*P*17). A superb panorama over the plain to Playa Blanca and out to Fuerteventura unfolds. You see the 'pimply' island of Lobos and the white dunes of Corralejo directly behind it. The hills tower above you, with ridges tumbling out of them in all directions.

Femés (118km ✗ 🎙) sits on a saddle overlooking the flat Rubicón plain. Your view is framed by the encircling hills. Take a break and enjoy the vista from this *mirador*. The church is dedicated to San Marcial, the island's patron saint, and the lovely church square is an ideal spot for a picnic if you don't want to huff and puff your way up the Atalaya! Femés is a precious little village, set high up in an already elevated valley and shut off from the rest of the island. Walks 17-20 converge on Femés (see photographs on pages 89 and 97-101). Continuing through fields, you drop down out of the valley and onto the LZ2. Cross straight over the main road and then continue straight ahead at the junction, on the narrower LZ30 (for *P*14 park 50m past the km22 stone).

Walks 14-16 set out from **Uga** (124km ✕), down to the left — a colourful village with a North African flavour about it. It rests in a saucer of gardens with its back up against the dark lava sea of the Timanfaya National Park. Walk 15 is a circuit; the other two descend to the coast.

Rounding a corner, the scenery changes yet again, as you enter the intriguing valley of **La Geria★**, a dark sweeping depression, further pitted with hollows. The slopes are coated in black ash. Myriad low half-moon stone walls *(zocos)* edge the hollows and stretch across the countryside (see photographs on pages 28-29 and 82). This is the home of *malvasía* wine, the product of an ingenious farming method: the vines are planted in crater-like depressions layered with *lapilli,* which absorb the dew and transport it down into the thirsty soil, thus enabling a single vine to produce up to as much as 200 kilos of grapes annually. *(Note: concentrate on the road; pull over when you want to 'ooh' and 'aah'.)* There are several *bodegas* along this road. At 130.5km ignore the right turn to Macher and, shortly after, a left turn to Tinajo. (This road to Tinajo is worth exploring one day, as is the road from El Grifo north to La Vegueta. Both are very scenic, with fine examples of *pahoehoe* lava.)

Leaving La Geria, you re-enter the lava — this time 'ropey' *pahoehoe* lava, characterised by surface ripples created when molten lava flowed beneath the solidified outer crust (see page 120). Strips of encroaching 'AA' lava, encrusted with lichen, give the effect of stagnant, weed-infested ponds. Cheerful green *Aeoniums* freckle the landscape. **Masdache** (135km ✕) lies amidst this upheaval of lava. Here's your chance to do some wine-tasting, at the Wine Museum on the outskirts of the village. But remember: you still have to drive home! A row of prominent, gaping craters lines the landscape on your right. Re-entering vineyards and vegetable gardens, serenity returns to the countryside. A couple of kilometres beyond Masdache, at a pretty, palm-filled junction, bear right for **San Bartolomé**, where you rejoin this morning's route and return to **Puerto del Carmen** (150km).

Walking

Lanzarote may not be your top choice for a walking holiday, but you may be as surprised as I was to find what this island has to offer walkers and nature lovers.

The walks in this book cover a good cross-section of the island. Do them all, and you will almost know Lanzarote inside-out. Almost — because, in a very commendable attempt to preserve the beauty of the island, the government will not permit you to explore throughout the Timanfaya National Park on your own; to see the best of it you'll have to join a guided walk.

There are walks in this book for everyone — take your pick after reading 'Organisation of the walks' on page 40.

Guides, waymarking, maps

You won't need a **guide** for any walk in this book except Walk 24 in Timanfaya: see above and page 116.

Waymarking/signposting is evident throughout the island these days, with fingerposts signalling both walking and mountain bike routes. Walks are being developed all the time — by local councils and the island government. There are **PR trails** (*pequeños recorridos;* short, day walks, waymarked yellow/white); **SL trails** (*senderos locales;* 'local' walks under 10km long, waymarked green/white); and the Canaries-wide **GR131** (*grande recorrido;* red/white-waymarked long-distance hike). This last is now complete: some 70+ km long, it runs in five stages from Orzola south to Playa Blanca. Eventually it is hoped to develop a long-distance **GR135** to encircle the island along the coast (200km). The *style* of waymarking is the same on all trails: single or parallel stripes indicate 'continue this way'; right-angled stripes herald a 'change of direction'; 'X' means 'wrong way'. ***We've added all routes known at time of writing if they fall within the area of our walking maps,*** but information about the newest trails had not yet been documented by the authorities at press date.

The **maps** in this book have been adapted from the 1:25,000 maps of the Servicio Geográfico del Ejército, updated in the field. For GPS users we have overlaid a UTM (28R) projection with 1km grid squares, Datum WGS84. Enquire at your local map stockist if you want the latest island maps at either 1:25,000 or 1:50,000.

Where to stay

Most of you will be staying in one of four places: Puerto del Carmen, Costa Teguise, Playa Blanca (ideally located for ferries to Fuerteventura), or Puerto Calero. Any of these bases is fine if you have a hire car or don't mind travelling via Arrecife and changing buses. But if you are going to Lanzarote mainly for a walking holiday, and you don't plan to hire a car, the best base is Arrecife, from where you can easily get to all the walks by local bus.

Each of the four main resorts is within easy reach of a solid week's walking, and you will find that by sharing a taxi one way and taking a local bus for the other part of the route (since you can usually get a bus at least one way), the cost of getting to and from walks is reasonable.

Finally, if you want something different, consider staying in a small countryside hotel or self-catering cottage. For these rural tourism options, see www.lanzarote.com.

What to take

If you don't have any special equipment, you can still do some of these walks, but don't attempt the more difficult ones without the proper gear. For each walk in the book, the *minimum* equipment is listed. You may find the checklist below useful — while bearing in mind that I've not done *every* walk in this book under *all* weather conditions. Use your good judgement to modify my equipment list according to the season!

walking boots	up-to-date transport timetables
waterproof rain gear	lightweight water containers
mobile phone (the emergency	extra pair of socks
number throughout all	long trousers
of Europe is 112)	long-sleeved shirt
bandages and band-aids	protective sun cream
plastic plates, cups, etc	knives and openers
windcheat	fleece, spare bootlaces
insect repellent	plastic groundsheet
sunhat, small rucksack	whistle, compass, torch

Weather

With an average annual temperature of 21°C and less than 140mm (5 1/2 inches) of rain per year, Lanzarote has about 345 days of sunshine. The winter months (November to March) are best for walking, but even then the days can be hot. Temperatures average 14-21°C in winter and 18-28°C in summer, with humidity between 60-70%. Good news for windsurfers: Lanzarote is a *windy* island, and the average water temperature is 20°C.

The prevailing wind is the *alisio* — the northeast trade wind. When this is blowing, the weather will be stable and generally fine. You may strike a few bad days, but the only place where the trade winds could ruin your day would be in the north, where low cloud might prevent you from appreciating those superb seascapes. It is very rare for rain to disrupt an entire day on the island. It usually lasts for only an hour or two, and then the sun shines again — at least on the coast.

If, however, the wind swings from northeast to southeast, a *calima* will blow in from Africa. This wind carries fine particles of sand from the Sahara and dumps them everywhere. At best the day will be hazy, but if the *calima* is blowing strongly, it's advisable *not* to go out walking: it may be difficult to see even a few hundred metres in front of you — the atmosphere will be so full of sand — or even stand upright! Obviously it causes havoc for contact lense wearers and is a danger to those with respiratory problems; headaches can affect anyone. The locals hate a strong *calima* because it affects tourism badly, especially any sea trips: the small boats can't go out in the rough weather, and even the large ferries cannot dock.

Nuisances

Dogs should not pose any problem on the island; all the 'working' dogs are either chained up or attended by their owners. **Mosquitoes** will keep you awake at night; be sure to apply ample anti-mosquito cream to keep them at bay. There are no other nuisances of the animal or insect variety, but in recent years **jeep safaris** have become popular, and you may find yourself eating dust on a few walks. Fortunately, in their frenetic search for quick thrills, they never stay in one place very long.

Spanish for walkers and motorists

In the tourist centres you hardly need know any Spanish. But out in the countryside, a few words of the language will be helpful, especially if you lose your way.

Here's an — almost — foolproof way to communicate

From left to right: lampranthus and Rumex vesicarius *(dock family) flourish near the coast; aeoniums abound from 100-800m. The ice plant* (Mesembryanthemum crystallinum) *is another coastal dweller.*

in Spanish. First, memorise the few short key questions and their possible answers, given below. Then, when you have your 'mini-speech' memorised, always ask the many questions you can concoct from it **in such a way that you get a 'sí' (yes) or 'no' answer**. *Never* ask an open-ended question such as 'Where is the main road?'. Instead, ask the question and then suggest the most likely answer yourself. For instance: 'Good day, sir. Please — where is the path to Máguez? Is it straight ahead?' Now, unless you get a 'sí' response, try: 'Is it to the left?'. If you go through the list of answers to your own question, you will eventually get a 'sí' response, and this is more reassuring than relying solely on sign language.

Following are the most likely situations in which you may have to practice your Spanish. The dots (…) show where you will fill in the name of your destination. Ask a local person — perhaps someone at your hotel — to help you with place name pronunciation.

Asking the way

Key questions

English	Spanish	approximate pronunciation
Good day, sir (madam, miss).	Buenos días, señor (señora, señorita).	**Boo**-eh-nohs **dee**-ahs, sen-**yor** (sen-yor-ah, sen-yor-**ee**-tah).
Please —	Por favor —	**Poor** fah-**vor** —
where is	dónde está	**dohn**-day es-**tah**
the road to …?	la carretera a …?	lah cah-reh-**teh**-rah ah …?
the footpath to…?	la senda de …?	lah **sen**-dah day …?
the way to …?	el camino a …?	el cah-**mee**-noh ah …?
the bus stop?	la parada?	lah pah-**rah**-dah?
Many thanks.	Muchas gracias.	**Moo**-chas **gra**-thee-ahs.

Possible answers

English	Spanish	approximate pronunciation
Is it here?	Está aquí?	Es-**tah** ah-**kee**?
there?	allá?	ayl-**yah**?
straight ahead?	todo recto?	**toh**-doh **rayk**-toh?
behind?	detrás?	day-**tras**?
right?	a la derecha?	ah lah day-**ray**-chah?

39

left?	a la izquierda?	ah lah eeth-kee-**er**-dah?
above?	arriba?	ah-**ree**-bah?
below?	abajo?	ah-**bah**-hoh?

Asking a taxi driver to take you somewhere and return for you, or asking a taxi driver to meet you at a certain place and time

English	*Spanish*	*approximate pronunciation*
Please —	Por favor —	**Poor** fah-**vor** —
take us to …	llévanos a …	l-**yay**-vah-nohs ah…
and return	y venga buscarnos	ee **vain**-gah boos-**kar**-nohs
at (place) at (time). *	a … a … .*	ah (place) ah (time).*

*Just point out the time on your watch.

Organisation of the walks

The book describes rambles all over the island. To choose a walk that appeals to you, you might begin by looking at the touring map inside the back cover. Here you can see at a glance the overall terrain, the roads, and the location of the walks. Flipping through the book, you will see that there is at least one photograph for every walk. Having selected one or two potential excursions from the map and the photographs, turn to the relevant walk. At the top of the page you will find planning information: distance/time, grade, equipment, and how to get there.

If the grade and equipment specifications are beyond your scope, don't despair! *There's almost always a short or alternative version of a walk,* and in most cases these are far less demanding. *If you want a really easy walk, you need look no further than the picnic suggestions on pages 10-15.* On the other hand, the hardy among you will find that Walk 2 will get you huffing and puffing! And there is always the opportunity to link several walks for a good day out.

When you are on your walk, you will find that the text begins with an introduction to the landscape and then turns to a detailed description of the route. The **large-scale maps** (all 1:50,000) have been annotated to show key landmarks. **Times** are given for reaching certain points in the walk. *Do* compare your pace with mine on one or two short walks, before you set off on a long hike. Don't forget to take bus connections into account!

Below is a key to the symbols on the walking maps:

▬▬▬	main road	🗗	best views	Ⅰ	pylon, wires
────	secondary road	✝	church.chapel	▪	specific building
────	tracks	†✚	shrine.cemetery	🚗	car parking
⁲→ ▰▰▰	route of the walk	⚲	spring, tank, etc	🚌	bus stop
⁲→ ▭▭▭	alternative route	P	picnic spot (see	⸋	A-A lava
⁲→ ·····	other walks		pages 10-15)	)	pahoehoe lava

Walk 1: AROUND LA GRACIOSA

See also photographs on pages 12 and 57

Distance: 19km/11.8mi; 6h

Grade: easy, gently undulating, but long. Can be very hot. *No shade*

Equipment: comfortable walking shoes, sunhat, light fleece, raingear, swimwear, suncream, picnic, plenty of water

How to get there and return: 🚌 to Orzola (Timetable 8), then ⛴ to La Graciosa (Timetables 18, 19). *Note:* the sea can be choppy!

Short walk: from Caleta del Sebo to the tidal lagoon (setting for Picnic 1) and back (2.5km/1.6mi; 45min). Easy. Heading out from Caleta del Sebo, turn off left for the cemetery (see map), which lies a little over 10min uphill. Then descend to the sea, bearing slightly right. In 8min, you'll reach the lagoon ... if the tide is in. This is a beautiful spot to spend the day if you don't want to walk far; the return along the seashore takes about 25 minutes. Note that there's little shade.

Alternative walk: You could follow coastal paths between **Caleta del Sebo and Playa del Ambar** (see map) — the distance is about the same, but it's somewhat slower going. The only disadvantage is that you might stop off at one of the pretty little beaches just at the start of the walk and go no further! Just north of Pedro Barba there is a blowhole and just north of Playa del Ambar an inlet bridged by four rock arches. In places the path is a bit eroded and vertiginous: you must be sure-footed

Note: There are two bicycle hire shops by the seafront.

All of you will have seen La Graciosa from the Mirador del Río. The vista is unsurpassed. For many people, this view from the *mirador* (shown below) is sufficient. But this little desert island deserves a second look. Take a ferry over and see for yourself. You'll discover superb beaches, sand dunes, lop-sided craters, and a lagoon. The fishing village, Caleta del Sebo, seems to be in perpetual slumber; a relaxing calm pervades. Getting there is fun in itself. The ferry passes through the straits of El Río in the shadows of the towering Famara cliffs.

La Graciosa from the Mirador del Río: the little port of Caleta del Sebo reaches out to sea, while the volcano Mojón rises in the background. Straight below lie the Salinas del Río.

Once you've got your legs back on steady ground again — on the quay at **Caleta del Sebo**, **head off** along the waterfront to the left. The village is a simple fishing haven of small low-slung houses. There are no gardens, no trees. Stark naked! At the end of the promenade, veer inland up past Bar/Pension Girasol Playa and onto a gravel road. Keep on this main inland route.

Out of the houses you cross a sandy/gravelly flat area, covered in various species of salt-resistant vegetation — *aulaga* (photograph page 99), *barilla* (the 'ice plant'; photograph page 39), *Schizogyne sericea* and *Traganum moquinii*. Looking back down the track, you have a superb shot over the village clustered along the water's edge to the dramatic Risco de Famara and the striking Playa del Risco (Walk 2), curving round the foot of the cliffs. On windy days you'll curse this dusty terrain. The two volcanoes, **Agujas Grandes** (right; also called **Pedro Barba**) and **Montaña del Mojón** (left), rise up ahead on either side of the track. A third, Montaña Clara (an island), soon appears in the background, centred between the other two.

At about **35min** you pass a fork off to the left around the north side of Montaña del Mojón. Shortly after, the track forks again (just in front of the village dump). Go right for Caleta de Pedro Barba. Reddish *cosco (Mesembryanthemum nodiflorum;* the red ice plant) brightens up the inclines here. Heading along the base of Agujas Grandes, your view stretches beyond the wall of cliffs to the Jable plain and the distant volcanoes of Timanfaya. Soon you cross a low crest and descend to a lower plain, edged by short, abrupt hills. Alegranza comes into sight, rising up out of the sea into an impressive table-topped mountain trailed by a tail of hills. The remains of stone walls come as a surprise out here. What could they have grown?

At about **1h40min** come to a branch-off left — your continuation, which circles the island. But why not first visit the beautifully-kept little port: stay on the main track and head to the right; it's only about 10 minutes to **Caleta de Pedro Barba** (**1h50min**). All the fishermen's old cottages here have been given glamourous 'facelifts'. Gardens filled with palms and shrubs encircle them, and a sandy cove sits just below. The good-sized jetty, which encloses a pool, points to the fact that this is no ordinary weekend retreat — it's a lovely serene spot with a good outlook over the cliffs and to Orzola.

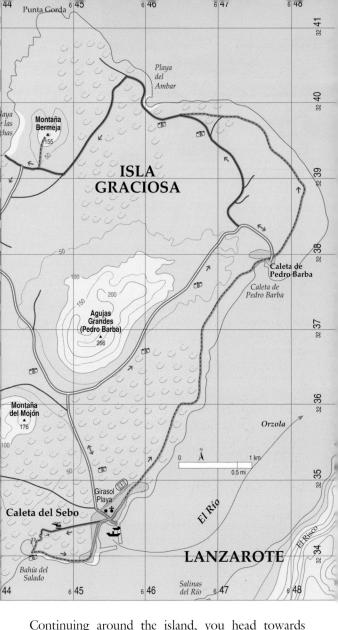

Continuing around the island, you head towards Alegranza on a rougher track. The north coast is sandier; dunes grow into the landscape. Ignore the faint forks off to the right within the next 15 minutes. *Polycarpaea nivea*, a dense, silvery-leafed plant, grows in the dunes. *Suaeda vera* crowns the little ant hills of sand that cover the plain. Montaña Bermeja, the 'Red Mountain', soon appears on

Playa de las Conchas rests at the foot of the maroon slopes of Montaña Bermeja. This clean beach of golden sand drops deeply into a blue sea.

your left, and Montaña Clara reappears, seemingly joined to the island.

At about **2h40min** the track forks; keep left and head towards the dunes to make for **Playa del Ambar**. What appears at first to be a lovely beach soon becomes a disappointment — it's littered with washed-up rubbish. Moreover, the rocks beneath the water's surface make swimming here awkward. The setting, however, makes an appealing photograph — the white dunes, green sea, and the volcanic hues of the mountains in the background. Don't worry — a better beach is en route! *Note: the west-coast beaches are usually treacherous; take care when swimming!*

The track heads behind and above the beach, fading as it crosses the dunes. Just after dropping down to the shoreline, you meet your turn-off, about 1h from the Caleta de Pedro Barba junction — a *very faint* track striking off left; it quickly becomes more obvious. Don't continue straight on; that way leads to Punta Gorda.

Shortly you're alongside **Montaña Bermeja**. The dunes lose their strength and flatten out, and Agujas Grandes now reveals its crater. Further along, the Timanfaya side of Lanzarote comes into sight. Coming alongside the southern flanks of Montaña Bermeja, take the track to the right. If you're pushed for time you may decide to forego the ascent to the summit and make straight for **Playa de las Conchas**, the exquisite beach shown above (**4h10min**).

From the beach, return to the wide main track (**4h 20min**) and keep ahead... past a large rubbish dump. It's a gentle ascent over a low col littered with stones and rocks. Ignore all branch-offs. Heading between the two craters, the Risco reappears like a green curtain in a theatre, bringing an end to the walk. When you rejoin your outgoing track, turn right for the port. There are plenty of pleasant places to relax and have some refreshment in **Caleta del Sebo** (**6h**), while you wait for the ferry to sail.

44

Walk 2: RISCO DE FAMARA

Distance: Access is best for motorists. Travelling by 🚗, allow 9.5km/ 6mi; 3h. By 🚌, the nearest stop is Máguez: 18km/11.2mi; 5h30min. Or get off the bus in Haría and pick up a taxi (that's how I've described the walk): ask the driver to take you to the parking place for motorists, but walk on to Máguez at the end for a 🚌 (14km/8.7mi; 4h30min).

Grade: very strenuous — a steep, gravelly descent/re-ascent of 450m/ 1475ft down a cliff face, with a possibility of vertigo for inexperienced walkers. No shade en route: the return is sheer slog. Don't attempt in wet weather. *Only recommended for experienced and fit walkers.*

Equipment: walking boots, sunhat, light jacket, raingear, swimwear, suncream, picnic, plenty of water

How to get there and return: 🚗 Travelling by car, park southwest of the Mirador del Río: descending from the *mirador* as in Car tour 1, watch for two derelict stone buildings just below the road on the right, 2.3km from the *mirador*. Just past them and just before the large Finca La Corona on the left, turn right on a narrow stone-paved track. Follow this track 100m to a small car park. Coming from the south, the track is on the left, just past the Finca La Corona. Or 🚌 to/from Máguez (Timetable 6; 'Sociedad' stop) and walk north to the starting point (see map and add 1h to the times below). Or 🚌 to Haría (Máguez bus; alight at the 'Plaza' stop) and then taxi: see under 'Distance' above.

This is a truly spectacular walk. You descend into the landscape viewed from the Mirador del Río and zig-zag steeply down the sheer Risco (cliff) de Famara. You discover that the captivating beach that sits imbedded in the lava tongue hundreds of metres below you is accessible after all! In the early morning and in the evening, this setting is no less than an oil painting. You'll probably want to make this an all-day hike, so do be prepared for the lack of shade.

Alight from the Máguez bus in Haría and pick up a taxi in the plaza. Ask the driver for 'Las Casillas', the name on the bus stop at the southern end of the road descending

The glowing ponds of the Salinas del Río

from the Mirador del Río. **Set out** by heading up this narrow cliff-top road, passing low lichen-clad stone walls criss-crossing countryside clothed in fig trees and prickly pear.

Your first turn-off comes up after 500m/yds, just metres past the large FINCA LA CORONA: take the stone-laid track off left, immediately before this wall. A stunning panorama slowly unravels, as you near the cliff-tops. You look straight out on to La Graciosa, bare of vegetation, desolate, and yet quite beautiful in the eyes of many beholders. The fishing village of Caleta del Sebo nestles around the exposed shoreline. Montaña Clara is the blade of rock that bursts up out of the sea behind La Graciosa and, further afield, to the right, lies the hilly island of Alegranza.

When the track ends in a small CAR PARK, continue straight on, now descending a rocky, sometimes stepped, path. Standing on the very edge of the cliff (Picnic 2), you look along a sheer wall of rock that plummets to a flat shelf below. Playa del Risco steals your attention with its golden sand and shallow turquoise-green water. Another sight distracts you: the strangely-coloured pink and maroon (and sometimes orange) ponds of

The fabulous Mirador del Río and the Famara cliffs

abandoned salt pans — the Salinas del Río.

The path swings down to the right of a magnificent VIEWPOINT by a POWER PYLON. The zigzag path demands keen attention, but no stretches of it are really vertiginous. An astonishing amount of vegetation clings to these cliffs, which harbour the richest plant life on Lanzarote. A number of very rare species, as well as nearly all the island's endemics are found in this northern massif. In and around these *riscos* you can find *Pulicaria canariensis*, *Asteriscus schultzii*, *Aichryson tortuosum*, *Kickxia*, *Reichardia*, two species of *Aeonium*, *Limoniums*, the rare *Echium decaisnei*, a yellow-flowering *Argyranthemum*, and many different grasses.

The desert-like Jable plain and the assortment of volcanic cones that constitute the Timanfaya National Park soon become visible over to the left. Approaching the faint track that cuts across the sea-flat below, you meet a fork: keep right. Join the track and turn right. (A left turn here used to lead to one of my favourite walks — down along the cliffs to Famara — but the trail is badly broken now and too dangerous to be recommended.) Looking back up the way you came, you're bound to be impressed. Moreover, you know that at least here you can escape the press of tourists. Five minutes along, clamber across a dry, gouged-out stream bed. Five minutes later, the track passes through a stone wall. Some 100m/yds *before* the wall, fork off left to the **Playa del Risco** (**1h**). Nirvana! At last you can fling off your clothes (hoping that the telescope at the Mirador del Río isn't trained on you …) and plunge into the cool sea.

Now, whether you decide to swim first *(watch out for broken glass)* or explore the salt pans, your continuation is along this lovely stretch of beach. La Graciosa is just across the strait — almost within swimming distance. At the end of the beach, scramble over the stones and rejoin your track, following it to its end (by an electricity transformer station). The cliffs stand before you — a formidable barrier of rock. See if you can locate the *mirador* in the cliffs above: this will show you just how well camouflaged it is.

From the track make your way over to the **Salinas del Río**, again watching out for broken glass. Pass the remains of a DERELICT BUILDING (**1h30min**). Towards the end of the salt pans you come to the second 'sight' of the walk: a magnificent pink, milk-of-magnesia-coloured pond enclosed by crumbling stone walls (photograph opposite). On a fine day you have a clear reflection of the Risco in it. On occasions the pools of the shallower pond in front of it glow a brilliant orange (see photograph on page 45).

Return by crossing a WALKWAY that circles the pink ponds, cutting across the salt pan. Rejoin the track some 12 minutes back, then keep left along it. When it fades out a few minutes on, veer left uphill — you'll find it becomes clear again. Turn right at a T-junction and remain on the track until you reach your outgoing descent path, then retrace your steps up the cliff.

When you're within sight of the top POWER PYLON (**3h 30min**), either keep uphill to your car or make for Máguez to catch a return bus. For the latter, head south on a somewhat vertiginous old path that hugs the edge of the cliff, taking in the last of this memorable view and passing a stone-covered house on your left. You scale the side of a ridge. Soon you come on to a track; follow it up over the crest, below a white house. Ignore all branch-offs. Descending now, the craters visited in Walk 6 dominate the Guinate Valley below you. When you reach the main road, turn right. The PLAZA/BUS STOP in **Máguez** lies 40 minutes downhill (**4h30min**).

Walk 3: FAMARA CIRCUIT

See photograph on page 123

Distance: 10km/6.2mi; 2h30min (motorists could save 2km/30min)

Grade: fairly easy, with an ascent/descent of about 130m/425ft, but not a walk for windy days when sand blows everywhere! *No shade en route*

Equipment: comfortable walking shoes, jacket, sunhat, raingear, suncream, picnic, plenty of water

How to get there: 🚌 (Timetables 13, 14) or 🚗 to/from La Caleta de Famara (to save 2km/30min, motorists can park near the *urbanización*)

Ondamentals one of my favourite walks has always been the descent of the Famara cliffs from the junction with Walk 2 to La Caleta, but it recent years it has become far too dangerous; landslides have broken the path in at least two places, and walkers have had to be rescued by helicopter.

Start the walk from the BUS STOP in **La Caleta**. Stroll over to the holiday houses and turn right up the road in front of them (signed 'Playa'). Despite being designed to resemble half-moon *zocos,* I find these bungalows ugly. But the track turns left once past them, and you have the wonderful sweeping view shown on page 123. When the track turns left down to the beach, walk ahead past a FARM wreathed in palms and then a walled THRESHING CIRCLE.

Eventually you rise to a locked *galería;* **1h10min**), where they have bored into the cliffs for water. The wealth of plants sprouting from the cliff walls testifies to the amount of moisture carried here by the northeasterly trade winds. Ahead is the way up the cliffs once used to access the salt pans. But this link with Walk 2 is too dangerous now; instead, turn left down a skiddy path behind the house and, at the T-junction, turn left on a track.

You pass an old PUMP HOUSE and the whole way back is easy walking. Although you'll be constantly entertained by the antics of the windsurfers, don't forget to look back to those inspiring cliffs! Perhaps finish off your day with a good fish meal in **La Caleta** (**2h30min**).

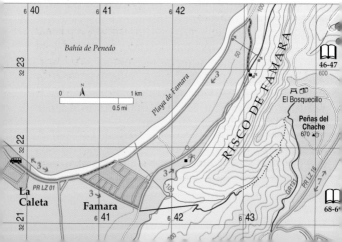

Walk 4: FROM MÁGUEZ TO YE

See map pages 46-47

Distance: 9.5km/6mi; 3h (or, if returning to Máguez: 14km/8/7mi; 4h10min)

Grade: moderate, with ascents of about 250m/820ft overall (of which 175m/575ft is at the end of the walk). Can be cold and misty.

Equipment: comfortable walking shoes, jacket, sunhat, raingear, sun-cream, picnic, plenty of water

How to get there: 🚌 to Máguez (Timetable 6; 'Sociedad' stop) or 🚗: park as for Picnic 4 on page 12, joining the walk at the 15min-point. *To return:* pre-arranged 🚗 taxi from Ye (Haría taxis: ☎928-835368, 928-529806 (English spoken), or 629-331827 (English spoken). Or walk the 5km back to Máguez (add 1h10min): head south from Ye on the LZ10, then turn right on a track opposite the Guinate road; follow this to your outgoing track, turn right and retrace your steps to your parked car or the bus stop in Máguez.

O n this pleasant countryside ramble you wind your way amidst the hills of the Famara massif — the highest and (in winter) the most lush corner of the island. Farm plots keep you company. Masses of solid stone walls fortify the inclines. In spring the herbaceous slopes are flecked with dandelions, indigo *Echium,* gold-coloured *Asteriscus,* white *Argyranthemum,* and mauve and scarlet poppies. A splendid sight! The massive yawning craters of Monte Corona and La Quemada, and the neighbouring Malpais (badlands) de la Corona remind you of the volcanic origins of Lanzarote.

The walk begins at the small PLAZA in **Máguez**, where the bus stops at an intersection. Follow the road diagonally across from you, the one that heads straight into the village (signposted 'Correos, Colegio, Sta B.bra'). A minute along pass the church square on the left. Two-three minutes later (after 150m/yds) turn left at an intersection. Ascending steadily (keep straight uphill) you look back over the village, spread along a gentle valley sprinkled with palms. Some 8 minutes up, a road joins you from the right. Just past it, branch off right on a farm track lined with palms (**15min**).

You exit through hills into another valley. Keep left at the fork several minutes along, crossing a saucer-shaped valley dominated by the enormous crater of 4000-year-old Monte Corona (609m/1995ft; photograph overleaf). A rough patchwork of cultivated fields stretches across the sloping inclines. Anywhere along this track is a lovely setting for Picnic 4.

Just over **35min** from Máguez go over an intersection at the foot of **Monte Corona**. A short way past here, there's a WATER TANK on the left with a faded blue door.

Some 400m/yds past the intersection, come to a second WATER TANK, just after a crossing cinder track (**40min**). *(Walk 5 sets off here for the ascent of Monte Corona.)*

From a col 300m/yds further on, the large, dilapidated castle-like house shown on page 21, the **Torrecilla del Domingo**, captures your attention. It sits high atop a ridge overlooking the northeastern inclines and the sea. On the slopes of Corona you see a plethora of colourful vegetation. But all colour drains out of the landscape as you approach ash-covered fields and a vast labyrinth of stone walls. Off the hillside, keep left at a fork and enter this labyrinth.

Close to the MIRADOR DEL RIO ROAD, at around **1h05min** into the walk, the track forks. Bear left. On reaching the road, keep straight ahead (left). A gap in the crater walls above gives you a good view of its sharp-toothed crown and an uninterrupted vista over the spiky interior of the **Malpais de la Corona**.

At the top of the rise, where the road curves left, veer off right through a gap in the roadside barrier on a wide farm track flanked by high stone walls and descend towards the *malpais*. Ignore two chained-off tracks turning off to the right but, where a wide farm track

sweeps down the hill in front of you, follow it to the right. Your route now circles another extinct volcano (La Quemada), which soon reveals a quite substantial crater. Looking back up the hillside you get a dramatic shot of Monte Corona: its razor-sharp rim rears up above the wall-rutted slopes.

At **1h35min** meet the ORZOLA ROAD and turn left, continuing along the edge of the *malpais*. Some seven minutes downhill, on a bend to the right, turn left on a track that circles **La Quemada**. A steady, sometimes steep climb will take you up to Ye. Ignore two private, chained-off tracks to the left. You sidle up against the mountain and get a glimpse of the inside of the crater. You cross the saddle, passing a house on the left. Ignore a track off left just past it. Descending, a deep valley slicing back into the plateau comes out of hiding. Your route dips down and crosses it. Ignore all side tracks as you head past beautifully cultivated land adorned with whimsical cacti.

At **2h40min** you ascend into another, higher valley, just below the plateau, and come into **Ye**, a small village sitting with its back to the gaping crater of Monte Corona. Cross the ROAD TO THE MIRADOR DEL RIO and pick up the road heading right, into the CENTRE (**3h**). This is

where your pre-arranged taxi from Haría should be waiting.

But you have a couple of options if you want to walk back to Máguez. You can head south on the LZ10 as far as the Guinate road, then head east on a track (as described on page 51), or you could return to your outgoing track via Monte Corona. A well-defined path leads from Ye to the lowest part of the crater. See the notes for Walk 5 and the various paths on the map.

Anywhere along the track, looking towards Monte Corona, is a good place to enjoy Picnic 4.

Walk 5: MONTE CORONA (MAGUEZ)

Distance: 7.2km/4.5mi; 2h25min

Grade: fairly strenuous ascent/descent of about 350m/1150ft, but only recommended for very experienced walkers; you must be sure-footed and have a head for heights (danger of vertigo)

Equipment: walking boots, jacket, sunhat, raingear, suncream, picnic, water

How to get there and return: 🚌 to/from Máguez (Timetable 6; 'Sociedad' stop) or 🚗: park as for Picnic 4 on page 12, joining the walk at the 15min-point. (See also the notes in the first paragraph below: you may prefer to park at the church in Ye and approach the crater from the north; this route *is* shown on our map, highlighted in violet.)

Monte Corona, one of the most impressive sights in the north of the island, dominates the horizon when approached from the south — from Máguez. It's certainly the highlight of Walk 4, as you can see in the photograph on pages 52-53. In the past, intrepid, sure-footed hikers have used Walk 4 as a starting point for the ascent. These days, judging by all the tracks on Google Earth, a more popular approach seems to be from Ye — an easier option via the collapsed northern rim of the crater. The ascent is 100m/330ft less than in my approach. Try it if you like:

take the southbound dirt track off the LZ201 at the km4 road marker, 150m east of the car park for Ye's church. Surprisingly, at press date this was still not signposted.

Otherwise, **start the walk** in **Máguez** by following Walk 4 (page 51) to the SECOND WATER TANK (**40min**). Turn left on the cinder track on the left-hand side of this tank. When the track ends in stone walls and terraced fields of cacti, head above the fields. In some places rainwater has eroded a 'path', but basically just make your way straight up to the top (a climb of just under 300m/1000ft). Where possible avoid the scree and keep to the volcanic rock all the way to the top of **Monte Corona** (**1h20min**) with its fantastic views round the clock. But, like me, you may be too mesmerised by the view almost 200m/650ft down *into* the crater to notice them at first.

If you've made it this far you no doubt have a very good head for heights and may decide to circle the crater's rim. I've not done so: my timings are simply out and back to **Máguez** (**2h25min**). Allow more time if you try any of the traces shown on the map — or forge your own!

Walk 6: MÁGUEZ • GUINATE • MÁGUEZ

Distance: 10km/6.2mi; 3h35min

Grade: moderate, but with a steep ascent of 300m/1000ft at the start of the walk.

Equipment: comfortable walking shoes, jacket, sunhat, raingear, suncream, picnic, plenty of water

How to get there and return: 🚌 or 🚐 (Timetable 6; 'Sociedad' stop) to/from Máguez

Alternative walk: Exclude the ascent to the trig point on Los Helechos, saving a climb of 100m and shortening the walk to 2h35min.

Short walk: Los Helechos (1.5km/1mi; 1h). A moderate climb of 100m/330ft; equipment as above. Access by 🚌 only. Use the notes below to leave Máguez on the lane followed in the walk. Drive (on surfaced road) to the white circular building and park. Pick up the notes at the 1h20min point. You'll be back at your car in 1h. Either drive back the way you came or, to enjoy the view shown below (right), continue the circuit on the motorable — if in places bumpy — track; you come out just above the Guinate Tropical Park.

Take it out! This summed up one reader's opinion of this walk — when it appeared as an alternative to Walk 4 in the first edition of the book. Why? Because part of the track had been surfaced, and the rest was motorable in any case. So we suggested on Update sheets that readers might like to omit this walk. And were pleasantly surprised by the response from other visitors. Not only did they urge us to leave it in the book, but to make it a walk in its own right — it's gorgeous, they said. Only farmers use the road and track, and the carpet of wild flowers in spring is a delight.

So we went to see for ourselves and decided that we

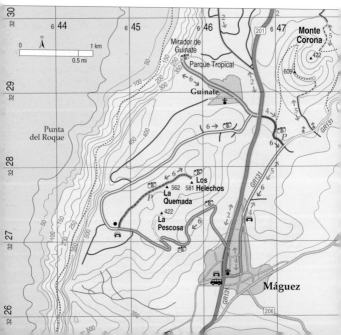

could please everyone. For those of you who abhor tarmac and tracks, but have a car, there's a delightful short walk to the twin craters of Los Helechos, from where you can enjoy one of the island's best views. But anyone wishing a longer walk, or limited to bus travel, can rest assured that this is *not* a busy road, and the only cars you are likely to see are those of the few local potato farmers.

And there's icing on the cake: Lanzarote has joined the elite circle of UNESCO's Geoparks, and this walk area is now a natural park, with information boards about local geology and agriculture all along the route.

To start out, head straight uphill from the BUS STOP in **Máguez**, following the GUINATE AND MIRADOR DEL RIO SIGNS. Just over 350m/yds along, fork half left up a narrow asphalted lane into the houses (CALLE DE LA CALDERA). As you climb, Monte Corona will catch your eye, well off to the right, but you are soon below the flanks of the Helechos volcano. About 1km along, the road curls to the left directly below Helechos, and you enjoy a fine view left down over Máguez. The ubiquitous *Nicotiana glauca* (photograph page 99) lines the road here as in so many other places on the island. Already you are approaching the fields of potatoes that characterise the higher sections of this walk.

Soon the road comes up to a rise, and the military installations atop the Peñas del Chache lie straight ahead in the southwest. Keep chugging uphill, ignoring all side-tracks; a new crater, La Pescosa, yawns ahead on the right.

La Graciosa, from above Guinate

A beautifully-walled potato plot marks the start of your short hike to La Quemada (left) and the trig point on Los Helechos (right).

A track veers off right to **La Pescosa**; ignore it and walk ahead to a circular white building with conical antennae behind it (a METEOROLOGICAL STATION; **1h20min**).

A cinder track turns right uphill just *before* the meteo building — your route to the trig point on Helechos. Even if you are omitting the climb to the summit, if you have a picnic, *do* carry on with the main walk for just a few minutes more. The track takes you up to the neatly walled-off potato plot shown above, with its own Lanzarote-green picket gate. Before you reach the end of the plot, head half-left on a grassy track/trail towards a plateau — yet another angle from which to enjoy 'the' perfect view of La Graciosa and the Risco cliffs (Picnic 6).

The main walk continues uphill to a small white building on **La Quemada** (562m/1845ft), past the gaping Pescosa crater on your right. From the house make for the trig point seen ahead: keep to the left of the white building and aim for the saddle between the hill you are on and the trig point. There is no path, but your way over the grass-covered hillside is obvious. Be sure to admire the pristine farm below in the valley, with its walled fruit trees.

Once on the ridge leading to the trig point, new views open up to Monte Corona and the Torrecilla del Domingo. Relax a while at the **Los Helechos** SUMMIT (581m/1905ft), overlooking Máguez straight below, with Haría beyond it and Arrieta and Mala stretching away down on the coast. Below you are twin craters, in

From top to bottom: pimpernels (Anagallis arvensis), mauve-flowering Canarian stock (Matthiola bolleana) and yellow Reichardia tingitana, storks's bill (Erodium), and a tangle of white and yellow cress (Cruciferae)

line with Monte Corona. One of them is well over 100m deep, and beautifully terraced.

Return to the METEORO-LOGICAL STATION (**2h20min**) and continue the circuit — now on a track. At a fork just past the station, keep right. Ignore all minor side-tracks. Eventually you descend into the **Guinate Valley** and will spot the Tropical Park below. You pass above the FARM seen from the climb to the trig point and soon enjoy a view to the Playa del Risco, reaching out towards the port at Caleta del Sebo. The narrow strait is a turquoise mirror. A wide grassy area on the left is another magnificent view-point, much beloved by local picnickers (see photograph on page 57).

Just under 1km further on you reach the GUINATE ROAD. Head left here, to visit the **Tropical Park**, or go right to the main road. Crossing the main road, take the track directly opposite. Turn right at an obvious right-angled bend and continue until you come to a T-junction with a cinder track. Turn right and follow this track (Walk 4 in reverse). Ignoring all side tracks, you come back into **Máguez** (**3h35min**). The bus leaves from the intersection by the PLAZA.

59

Walk 7: AROUND HARIA

See also photographs pages 1, 13, 18

Distance: 7km/4.3mi; 2h30min

Grade: easy, but sometimes slippery underfoot. A bit of scrambling through brambles. An initial descent of 220m/720ft, followed by an ascent/descent of 200m/650ft; you must be sure-footed and have a head for heights near the cliff-edge in the second half of the walk.

Equipment: comfortable walking shoes, sunhat, light jacket, raingear, long trousers, suncream, picnic, water

How to get there and return: 🚌 (Timetable 6; 'Plaza' stop) or 🚗 to/from Haría, then taxi to the Restaurante Los Helechos: (928-835368, 928-529806 (English spoken), or 629-331827 (English spoken). Note that the bus *goes through* Haría before returning to stop in the plaza.

Short walks

1 **Restaurante Los Helechos to Haría** (2.5km/1.5mi; 1h). Easy, but slippery underfoot when wet. Equipment, access/return as main walk. Do the first half of the main walk only.

2 **Haría — Valle de los Castillejos — Valle del Rincón — Haría** (4.5km/2.8mi; 1h30min). Grade, equipment as main walk. 🚌 or 🚗 to/from Haría. Do the second half of the main walk only. For a *very* short walk (45min in total), leave the Castillejos Valley by the track met at the 1h23min-point and return on the far side of the valley.

Alternative walks (see also map pages 68-69)

1 **Start the walk at the Ermita de las Nieves** (add 3km/2mi; 40min). From Haría, take a taxi to the *ermita*, and from there follow the (motorable) track northeast past the 'golf balls' of the Peñas del Chache to the main road. Then turn left downhill for 200m to the Restaurante Los Helechos, to pick up the main walk below. PR LZ 16

2 **Valle de Malpaso** (6.5km/4mi; 2h). Grade, equipment as main walk. 🚌 (Timetable 6; 'Plaza' stop) or 🚗 to/from Haría (or start at the Restaurante Los Helechos, if you're feeling particularly energetic). Start at the 1h-point of the main walk, at the church square in Haría. Follow the main walk to the 2h-point, the motorable track. Do not turn left here through the Valle del Rincón, but instead follow the somewhat wider track climbing gently up to the LZ10. Turn left downhill along the road and turn left again after just under 1km, through a gap in the roadside barrier (there is a signpost here for the PR LZ 16). You have now joined the main walk at the 30min point, where it crosses the LZ10 for the second time. (The energetic will see a similar gap in the roadside barrier leading uphill, if they want to head up to the Restaurante Los Helechos.) Follow the main walk past César Manrique's house, back to the church square in Haría.

T his delightful countryside ramble takes you down a centuries-old trail into the palm valley of Haría, with wonderful views all the way. After a break, you leave the village to walk up the Valle de los Castillejos, along the edge of the Famara cliffs, and then down the Rincón Valley back into the village. The ramble ends at the lively church square — the Plaza Leon y Castillo.

Pick up a taxi at the PLAZA in **Haría** and ask for the Restaurante Los Helechos. Circling up the impressively-

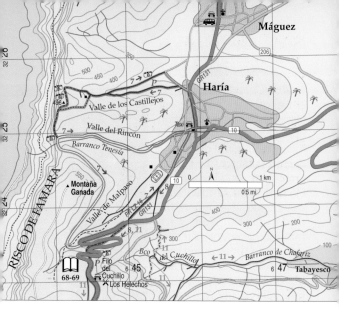

walled hairpins by taxi, you may wonder how you're going to get back down to Haría on an 'easy' path! After enjoying the view from the *mirador* at the restaurant, **start the walk** by heading down the road in the direction you've just come (passing the km17 stone), with the **Barranco del Cuchillo** a deep gash on your right. As you approach a sharp bend, there is a break in the roadside barrier on the right (just below electricity wires). Step through — into history. Stone paving underfoot recalls the days when this was the pilgrims' route from the north to the Ermita de las Nieves. This is the PR LZ 16, which runs between Haría and the Ermita de las Nieves (see Alternative walk 1).

You head straight for the white 'Mirador de Haría' building on the **Filo del Cuchillo** ('knife's edge') but, before you reach it, the path veers off to the left. All the way down (Picnic 7a), on a very gentle gradient, you enjoy long-range views over Haría ... while you step through a veritable botanic garden. You'll cross the road (*carefully*) three times. At the second crossing there's a sign, '**Valle de Malpaso**'). After the third crossing (**30min**), the way becomes a cart track, and you can pluck some wild fennel to add to your herbs if you're in self-catering accommodation. Monte Corona rises just to the left of the large school building. The plots of maize, potatoes, marrows and vines are festooned with huge fig trees.

On coming to a T-junction (**40min**) with a diagonally

61

On the descent from the mirador, *you look ahead to the two valleys explored in the second part of the walk.*

crossing track, head left towards the SCHOOL, soon passing an OLD FARM flanked by two palms and then some derelict cottages (the latter a rare sight on Lanzarote). Coming onto tarmac, keep straight ahead — ignore the road to the left. Now watch for the house on the left surrounded by trees and lava-stone walls: this was CÉSAR MANRIQUE'S HOUSE at the time of his death. At a Y-fork not far past it, bear right. Ignore side-streets. When you reach a square, keep left to continue. At the T-junction, where the town hall is on your right, turn right and immediately left and left again, back to the taxi rank and the CHURCH SQUARE in **Haría** (**1h**).

Moving on (perhaps after a quick drink), follow the main street north uphill, passing a restaurant on the right. Ignore a fork back left into the village in five minutes, but at a junction a minute later, go left: pass Calle Romero and head downhill on CALLE CASAS ATRAS. After about 100m/yds fork left up an earthen track with grass down the middle. Monte Corona is ahead to the right, with the green spread of Máguez below it. This delightful track through cultivation and wild flowers takes you up the **Valle de los Castillejos** (Picnic 7b; photograph page 18), where a dry *barranco* falls away gently on the right.

The bulk of Montaña Ganada looms ahead. To the left is a series of hillocks, with neatly-terraced 'aprons' of vine-yards. Pass a house (**1h20min**) and ignore tracks off left into fields. Three minutes later (**1h23min**) a track joins from the right. (For a very short walk, you could turn right and follow this track across the valley and back to the main road.)

By **1h30min** or less you're just below a RUIN and cinderblock gateposts leading to a stone-faced building. Continue uphill on the track. In five minutes the track

ends at a terraced plot. You've climbed up to the right (north) of a castellated ROCKY OUTCROP that rises just at the edge of the **Risco de Famara**.* To continue, walk between the two palm trees about 20m/yds away to your right. A faint path now becomes visible; follow it straight ahead towards the long, low stone wall that borders the edge of the cliff.

When you reach the cliff-edge, you will be astounded by the stunning views. But the views are even better from the very top of the outcrop on your left, so climb it, using the faint path (which some people may find vertiginous). From up here you're 'on top of the world': on the right is La Graciosa, Alegranza and Roque del Oeste. On the left, beyond the long golden beach of Famara, you can see the wastelands as far as La Santa and Sóo. On the horizon are the Montañas del Fuego, and behind you are Haría and Máguez.

From the top of the cliff follow the faint path downhill (it runs at a safe distance from the edge). The path takes

*If you find this section too vertiginous, go back inland towards the cinderblock gateposts and walk up the hill behind them, avoiding any private property. When you get to the top of the rise, keep right to join the path along the cliffs.

The Ermita de las Nieves (top left); view from the ermita *(bottom left) and César Manrique's simple grave in the cemetery at Haría*

you down to a small *mirador* with drystone walls and the (motorable) track (**2h**), where you turn left downhill through the **Valle del Rincón** — totally different in character from the Castillejos. There are no far-reaching views, fewer flowers, and little cultivation.

What catches the eye instead are the soft rosy-rusty hues emanating from the soil and the rock, set off by isolated splashes of cultivation. Notice, for instance, some 10 minutes down the track, a fruit tree on the right, completely enclosed by a circular drystone wall. On the hillsides opposite this tree, the stone walls not only help prevent erosion, but also capture water coming off the hillside and trap it in pools — at least in spring. Two minutes later a mini-reservoir on the left allows one lucky farmer to irrigate his smallholding; outside summer, pink carnations thrive among his marrows and onions. Around here the track is embroidered with ice plants (photograph page 39).

Looking south, you should be able to spot your descent route in the first part of the walk. A swathe of vegetation takes you back into **Haría**. Pass the SCHOOL on the right and come into a small grove of palms, where there is a ruin ahead. Bear left in front of the ruin, then ignore a road to the right. Continue on tarmac. Soon a *barranco* is just on the right. Go straight over all junctions until you come to the town hall and return to the PLAZA LEON Y CASTILLO (**2h30min**).

Walk 8: HARIA • RESTAURANTE LOS HELECHOS • ERMITA DE LAS NIEVES • TEGUISE

Map begins on page 61 and ends on pages 68-69; photographs opposite and on pages 1, 13, 25, 64, 70-71, 72

Distance: 14km/8.7mi; 4h30min

Grade: moderate but long, with an ascent of about 350m/1150ft.

Equipment: comfortable walking shoes, sunhat, long trousers, rain-gear, suncream, picnic, water, warm clothing (it can be cold and misty)

How to get there and return: 🚌 to Haría (Timetable 6; 'Plaza' stop)
To return: 🚌 from Teguise (Timetables 6, 7, 14)

This walk between two of the island's loveliest villages is characterised by spectacular vistas and a wealth of endemic flora. The ascent out of Haría almost goes unnoticed as you rise through a 'botanic garden' on an extremely well-graded mule trail, which was once the main route to the old capital, Teguise, as well as a pilgrims' path to the *ermita*. Once the ascent is over, you enjoy that 'top of the world' feeling and can just stride out.

Start the walk with your back to the TOWN HALL in **Haría**: turn left, then take the first left (CALLE EL PUENTE). The PR LZ 16, which runs from Haría to the Ermita de las Nieves, is signalled here by an INFORMATION BOARD and FINGERPOSTS. Keep straight ahead where a lane forks back to the right. The street becomes CALLE ELVIRA SANCHEZ and you pass (all on the right): CÉSAR MANRIQUE'S FORMER HOUSE (the ample grounds surrounded by volcanic stone walls), the SCHOOL AND SPORTS GROUND, a pair of derelict cottages and the solitary OLD FARM BUILDING shown on page 1.

At the next fork, keep right. You will now climb straight up across the hairpin bends of the LZ10. After the first road crossing the way narrows into the old stone-laid donkey trail. When you reach the road for the fourth time, turn up left to the RESTAURANTE LOS HELECHOS (**1h30min**) and perhaps take a break.

Continue along the LZ10 for another 200m/yds, then bear right on a road signposted 'MIRADOR RISCOS DE FAMARA'. Follow it below the **Peñas del Chache** (a military installation and off-bounds to the public) to the **Ermita de las Nieves** (**2h**; Picnic 9). The current building dates from 1966, but there has been a place of worship on this site since the 15th century.

From the *ermita*, use the notes for WALK 9 on page 69 from the 3h05min-point to continue to **Teguise** (**4h 30min**), the gem of a town described on page 26. The lively Sunday market is worth visiting during your stay.

See also photographs pages 25, 64, 70-71, 72. 74

Distance: 18.5km/11.5mi; 5h35min

Grade: strenuous, with a drawn-out ascent of 600m/1970ft in the first part of the walk. Can be quite cold, windy and misty ... or even wet!

Equipment: comfortable walking shoes, warm jacket, sunhat, raingear, suncream, picnic, plenty of water

How to get there: 🚌 to the 'Correos' stop in Mala (Timetable 6)
To return: 🚌 from Teguise (Timetables 6, 7, 14)

Shorter walks: both are easy; equipment as above. Take private transport (friends, or a taxi from Haría or Teguise) to start; return by bus.

1 **Ermita de las Nieves to Teguise** (8km/5mi; 2h30min). Pick up the main walk at the Ermita de las Nieves and follow it to the end. If you are travelling by 🚗, park in Teguise and take a taxi from there.

2 **Ermita de las Nieves to Mala** (10.5km/6.5mi; 2h30min). Pick up the main walk at the chapel and use the map to walk down to Mala; it's very straightforward — but see above notes on weather conditions. If you are travelling by 🚗, park in Mala and telephone the Haría taxi (see page 60); they will collect you in Mala and take you to the *ermita*; you pay *only* for the journey between Mala and the *ermita*.

Crossing the island from east to west, you climb to the solitary Chapel of the Snows (Ermita de las Nieves) — the coldest point on Lanzarote. So if you're after some bracing air ... join us and leave the sea plain! You wind up into a narrow concealed valley. The denuded clay-brown slopes soon fold up into pasture-like inclines (in winter and spring). Seascapes and mountain views accompany you all the way up to the chapel — where from a windswept plateau you enjoy a 360° panorama — the view of views.

When you leave the bus at **Mala** at the 'Correos' (post office) stop, **start by** heading north along the road. Several minutes along, turn up a road branching off left — where a road sign on the right depicts a MAN DESCENDING STEPS. Immediately the road forks: bear right. You pass the church shown above (**Nuestra Señora de la Merced**). The village is immersed in fields of prickly pear — sidle up to some of these plants to see the cochineal insects thriving on the gooey white cactus juice. You can see the wall of the Presa (reservoir) de Mala ahead, wedged across the mouth of the Valle del Palomo.

In about 300m/yds go over the LZ1 and ignore tracks on either side of the bridge, then continue straight ahead on a rough track. Some 100m/yds further on, when the track forks by two houses, go right. Your climb begins as you leave the farmland behind. Just before crossing the crest into the **Valle del Palomo**, you get a good view along the sea plain of Mala, buried under a dark green

66

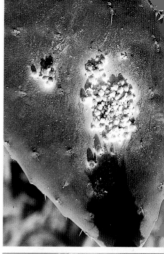

Nuestra Señora de la Merced is the little church passed at the start of the walk in Mala. Just beyond it, you come into prickly pear plantations, and have an opportunity to inspect the habitat of the cochineal insect at first hand.

cloak of prickly pear, and then the carpet of tightly-woven gardens extending back to Guatiza. Some 30-35 minutes uphill, ignore a fork right to a building. To see the fish pond-sized **Presa de Mala** (the only reservoir on Lanzarote), leave the track and cross the top of the crest; it's only a few minutes over the top.

Somewhat over 1km and 100m/300ft higher up the valley, you pass behind some houses … and continue climbing. After gaining another 100m in height, you cross the bed of the stream, and (outside summer) see before you a verdant valley. After the rains have fallen, this is the most luxuriant valley on Lanzarote. Higher still, and keeping always to the main track, you re-cross the bed of the *barranco* and the track lazily zigzags up out of the valley. Yellow, violet and scarlet flowers set the hillside alight. Catch a corner of the Malpais de la Corona (Walk 4) over the hills. Mounting the plateau, you swing up past a Lilliputian FARM dwelling leaning against a rocky nodule. A minute or two beyond the farmhouse you circle a house and, looking back, you have a fine view down onto Arrieta and the sea. To the northwest you see the plateau of Guatifay and the prominent cones of Corona and La Quemada (Walk 4). The great gap separating you from these craters is created by the valleys of Máguez and Haría — an impressive sight.

Meet the LZ10 (**2h30min**) and follow it to the left. Over to the right rises the island's highest summit, the Peñas del Chache, crowned by a large military installation. As you descend, the Llanos de Zonzamos (the sweeping plain behind Arrecife) comes into view, with Arrecife in

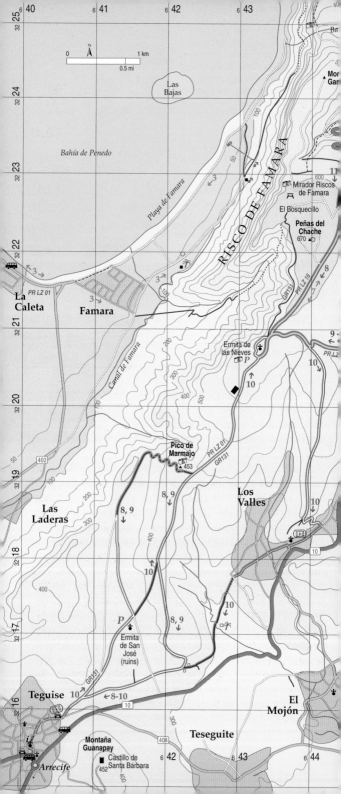

the background. The refuge of Las Nieves soon captures your attention. It stands conspicuously alone on the tableland. The signposted turn-off to it comes up in 800m/yds; head right. Los Valles is visible through the mouth of the *barranco* below. Soon the roar of the sea is heard, and a roadside *mirador* gives you a view over the Playa de Famara far below.

Once alongside the **Ermita de las Nieves** (**3h05min**; Picnic 9), you're probably getting a good battering from the wind. If this is the case, picnic inside the walls that enclose this haven. For an unparalleled vista, head over the cliffs *(carefully)*. Below you lies the beach of Famara. Beyond it, the desert-like Jable plain fans inland, littered with remnants of volcanoes. On your right, the Risco de Famara (Walk 2) ends abruptly in a razor-sharp tail; beyond lie the islands of Graciosa, Montaña Clara and Alegranza.

Once you've soaked up this great view, continue on the gravel road that descends south of the chapel and follow it along the crest of this declining ridge towards Teguise. The locals use this road, and the odd tourist will bounce past in a jeep. *(If you don't like sharing your walk with motor vehicles, after 2km follow the route highlighted in violet: at the 'Marmajo' fingerpost ascend a clear, sandy-coloured track on the right. From the rise look down straight below to a track behind a large rectangular field. It's an easy scramble down to this other track, which you follow to the left. Two kilometres outside Teguise, fork right to pass the substantial remains of the Ermita de San José (see map; Picnic 10).)*

Shortly the modest Castillo de Santa Bárbara becomes a prominent landmark. Set on the crater rim of Montaña Guanapay, it stands guard over Teguise and the encompassing plains. Following the main (motorable) track, you head back into fields. About 3km from the Ermita de las Nieves ignore the GR trail to the right. (This short-cut is used in Walk 10.) Then, about 1.5km further on, after a track joins from the left, you descend to an intersection. Here the track turns left to join the LZ10; you, however, keep straight on through the intersection. After 200m or so a track joins from the right. Some 12 minutes later, come to a wide track and follow it to the left.

Entering the rear of **Teguise**, now on asphalt, pass the STADIUM and come to a junction. Just keep straight ahead into the street with the 'no entry' sign. Then head half-left towards the church tower seen in this photograph. Follow the street down through houses and over a small bridge. Just over the bridge, cross a huge square to the CHURCH, **Nuestra Señora de Guadalupe**. An arched gateway lets you into a beautiful plaza. Exit to the left of the '**Bankia**' (if it's open, take a peep inside this well-restored building). You come out to another SQUARE (**5h35min**); catch your bus here, outside the **Convento de San Francisco** (which now houses the MUSEUM OF SACRED ART).

It's worth spending at least two hours exploring Teguise — a jewel of a town.

Walk 10: TEGUISE• LOS VALLES • TEGUISE

See map pages 68-69; see also photographs on pages 25 and 64

Distance: 16km/10mi; 4h30min

Grade: moderate but fairly long. Ascent/descent of about 270m/900ft overall. One short pathless descent. Can be cold, windy, misty, wet...

Equipment: comfortable walking shoes, warm jacket, sunhat, raingear, suncream, picnic, plenty of water

How to get there and return: 🚌 or 🚗 to/from Teguise (Timetable 6, 7, 14; 'Centro de Salud' stop). Motorists should park by the stadium on the eastern outskirts of Teguise. The 'Centro de Salud' bus stop is just south of the stadium: with your back to the bus shelter, turn right and walk towards the masts of the stadium (easily seen); see map.

This walk, a variation on Walk 9, is especially suitable for motorists. Non-motorists might like to do the walk on a Sunday, when there are extra buses running to Teguise for the popular market. Use the map to make your way to the stadium.

Start the walk at the STADIUM in **Teguise**. Referring to the map on pages 68-69, head northeast along the GR131 towards the Ermita de San José. The tarmac quickly gives way to track. In just **2min** you pass another motorable track coming in from the right — the final leg of Walks 8 and 9 (and your return route). At a Y-fork (**7min**), bear right. This takes you to the substantial ruins of the **Ermita de San José** (Picnic 10) on your right.

Just 60m/yds past the *ermita,* cross straight over a motorable track and follow the GR fingerposts along a

Not only palms surround the ruin in the valley south of Los Valles: it's choked with a collar of ancient prickly pear and fresh green verode.

lovely old mule trail going straight ahead uphill. Rejoining the motorable track route of Walks 8 and 9, you pass an ARMY TELECOMMUNICATIONS CENTRE and quickly come to the **Ermita de las Nieves** (**2h15min**).

Leave the *ermita* by heading east-southeast on the asphalt road towards the LZ10. After 10 minutes, on the first sharp left-hand bend, take the clear track straight ahead. Follow this for about 35 minutes, passing under cables, until the track splits three ways. Take the left-hand branch and zigzag down into **Los Valles** (**3h10min**). Turn right past the SPORTS COMPLEX, and at a three-way road junction (where the LZ10 is ahead to the left), turn sharp right, to pass a small CHURCH and SCHOOL on the right. Follow this road for 15 minutes, over two crossroads and eventually up a short incline out of Los Valles. There are cinder fields either side and the odd house.

Once past the last FARM on the left, with animal sheds and noisy, chained dogs (**3h25min**), ignore a track going left up to the top of the small hill. Now the walk continues pathless for a very short way. At this point you are on a right-hand bend in the asphalt road. Look down into the valley ahead and locate a ruined farm surrounded by palms. Just before and to the right of it is a faint track with walls either side. Carefully descend the open hillside to that track and follow it to the right of the FARM RUINS (**3h30min**).

From the ruin, *do not* follow the red soil track that sweeps left just in front of the building; keep to the stony track between the walls, crossing (or fording) a STREAM BED. The track rises diagonally left, but has been washed away in places, so climb above the right-hand wall and walk above the washed-out track until your onward track (now narrowed to a path) is clearly visible ahead, climbing the hillside. The path joins a track coming from the left at some CULTIVATION (**3h55min**). You walk between two sheds and join the MAIN JEEP TRACK between the Ermita de las Nieves and Teguise used in Walks 8 and 9. Follow this track back to the STADIUM in **Teguise** (**4h30min**).

See map pages 68-69; see also photographs pages 13, 64, 72

Distance: 12km/7.4mi; 4h (travelling by bus, add 2km/35min overall)

Grade: strenuous; an ascent/descent of about 500m/1650ft overall and a pathless descent requiring care. Can be cold, windy, misty ... or wet

Equipment: walking boots, warm jacket, sunhat, raingear, suncream, picnic, plenty of water; *strong gloves* (for the pathless descent on all fours)

How to get there and return: 🚗 or 🚌 to/from the 'Tabayesco' stop on the LZ1 (Timetables 6, 8). Park by the bus shelter in Tabayesco itself

Short walk: Barranco de Chafariz/del Cuchillo (5km/3mi; 2h; equipment and access as main walk; quite easy, with an ascent/descent of about 200m/650ft). Follow the main walk to the 40min-point. Take the left turn at this T-junction. This track soon becomes a grassy path as it sweeps round above your outward route. The view of the valley is wonderful — all the way to Arrieta on the coast — as the path runs between cultivated terraces. When you reach the LZ207 (54min) turn left and walk down this quiet road for eight-nine minutes. Cross a *barranco* on a bridge and immediately after take the clear track going left. This track, lined with palm trees, gives you a real feel for the valley, as it passes through vineyards and fruit orchards. You reach a junction (the 37min-point of your outward route; 1h12min). Turn right and retrace your outward route back to Tabayesco (1h50min).

This walk starts at Tabayesco and goes through a delightfully lush and fertile valley, using an old mule trail to join the Haría road (LZ10). From there the main walk continues up the mule trail to the mirador above the Restaurante Los Helechos, then follows the PR LZ 01 along a ridge between the Cuchillo and Palomo valleys. From there a pathless descent could take you down through terraces to join Walk 9 in reverse to end in Mala. But the main walk continues along the ridge. A final, tricky pathless descent takes you back down to Tabayesco.

Start out in **Tabayesco** by taking the lower (right-hand) road at the junction by the BUS SHELTER*, heading into the village. Ignore Calle la Luciana running left up to the church. At the end of the village (**8min**) the road becomes a wide dirt track rising up the valley. The Restaurante Los Helechos is already visible on the hilltop ahead and slightly to the left. Every bit of arable land is being cultivated with fruit, vines, vegetables or just animal food in this valley; it's lushly green and refreshing in spring. You may even be regaled by the song of a nightingale in April, although house buntings are more common here (an African bird similar to a small hedge sparrow but more musical).

Ignore tracks going off either side to fields or houses,

*This bus stop, called 'Tabayesco Pueblo' was disused at press date; bus travellers walk here from the 'Tabayesco' stop on the LZ1 (see map).

In the Valle del Palomo (Walk 9)

until you reach a major split in the tracks (**37min**). The left-hand track is the return route for the Short walk. Take the right-hand track and continue to ignore small tracks leaving this main track, which is always obvious as it heads straight up to the top of the valley. Just after passing tracks going off either side (the one to the left to a small house), you come to a T-junction (**45min**), where Restaurante Los Helechos is to the left. *(The Short walk goes left here.)*

The main walk goes right at this point, on a track which soon peters out into a path. This path — very unusually for Lanzarote — wades through waist-high grass in parts, and you need to dodge the odd cow pat. It affords fabulous views down the valley. You reach a stone-laid mule trail, clearly marked by red paint dots and/or cairns. Follow the zigzags and the going is easy. In a further 12 minutes you reach the top. Here you meet a track and, turning left for 100m/yds, you come to the LZ207 road (**1h10min**). Go right for 50m, to the LZ10, from where you look down into the Haría and Máguez valleys and see the Risco de Famara ahead. A track directly opposite would take you into Haría in 10 minutes if you wished.

But for the main walk, continue along the road to the left (carefully) for a good five minutes. Less than 150m beyond the km20 marker, head left uphill on a mule trail (**1h15min**). This lovely trail (the PR LZ 16, followed in Walks 7 and 8) leads you easily up past the hairpins on the road, passing the white 'Mirador de Haría' building at the **Filo del Cuchillo** ('knife's edge'; **1h40min**), with wonderful views down the valley through which you have just walked. After two more crossings, including one close to the Restaurante Los Helechos, you meet a track. You are now above the restaurant.

Turn left on this track, parallel to the LZ10 below you at the km17 marker. The military base at Peñas del Cache is ahead to the right and, as you meet another road leading to the Ermita de las Nieves, walk over to a ROADSIDE VIEWPOINT to your left on the LZ10 (**1h55min**). You have walked from not far above sea level at Tabayesco to the highest point on the island, and the fabulous views are a great reward. You can see the restaurant on your left, with Montaña Corona beyond; behind you is Peñas del Cache and the Ermita de las Nieves; in front is the Valle del Cuchillo/de Chafariz, with Tabayesco and the coast at Arrieta beyond; to the right is the ridge separating this valley from the Valle del Palomo (Walk 9).

Note now a track along this ridge, which begins beyond some palm trees on your right about 650m away. This track is your onward route. Follow the LZ10 south, walking carefully, to meet this track. Just after the last roadside palm, 100m after the km16 marker and just past a house on the left, take the track which initially runs parallel to the road, to its left. It then turns away from the road (by a PR LZ 01 WAYMARKING POLE; **2h05min**), running towards the ridge you saw. You pass between potato fields and, as the ridge narrows, you start to see the Palomo Valley on your right as well as the Cuchillo/ Chafariz Valley to the left. The track up the Palomo Valley followed in Walk 9 is clearly visible. When the track forks, go right (left goes to a house). Heading out along the ridge, you pass the odd building and ruin. Anywhere beside the track makes a beautiful picnic spot with far-reaching views over the Palomo Valley or back to the

Picnic 11: On the ridge between the valleys of Palomo (right) and Cuchillo, north of Peña de la Pequeña

Peñas de Chache. *(You could link up with Walk 9 and follow it in reverse to end up in Mala. The outward track used in Walk 9 is clearly visible below, and the pathless descent via abandoned terraces is easily negotiable in 15 minutes. You would join the track in the 'verdant valley' near the barranco crossings at approximately the 2h-point on that walk.)*

Continuing the main walk along the ridge, you come to a Y-fork with a PR LZ 01 FINGERPOST at **Peña de la Pequeña (2h35min)**, indicating a left turn. Encouraging as this is, it's the last waymarking until Tabayesco! Follow the track left along the ridge, to come to potato fields at **Cerro Tabayesco**. Beyond here the track deteriorates and becomes *very* indistinct. You need to leave the ridge and head down to Tabayesco. Fortunately — despite the authorities warning that this part of the trail is three-star difficult and yet neglecting to mark it even with sighting posts — navigation is easy. Locate Arrieta (the final goal of PR LZ 01) on the coast — it's the first village you can see; the one further left (north) is Punta de Mujeres.

Now scramble *carefully* straight down this gentle but very skiddy and eroded, ankle-twisting slope towards Arrieta, weaving and picking your way over the terraces and gullies, sometimes on all fours (gloves come in handy!). You should brush past a RUINED HOUSE hard on your left, then make for the LZ207 below. When you come to a few plots just above the road, be sure to pass to the left (top) of them, or you'll have to fight your way through prickly pear. Join the road (at a PR LZ 01 WAY-MARKING POLE!; **3h40min**) and go right, back to the disused BUS SHELTER at **Tabayesco (4h)**.

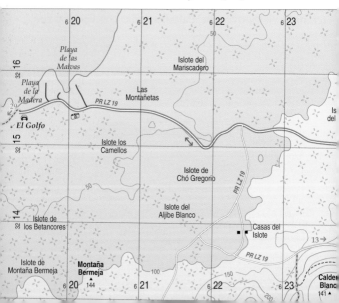

Walk 12: MANCHA BLANCA • PLAYA DE LA MADERA • TINAJO

Distance: 21.5km/13.3mi; 5h20min

Grade: easy but long. Since there is no shade en route, this walk is not recommended in very hot weather. Note also: if you plan to swim in the rock pools or at the beach, make absolutely certain that the sea is safe. I have never swum at the beach myself, because it never looked safe enough to me!

Equipment: comfortable walking shoes, fleece, sunhat, raingear, suncream, swimwear, picnic, plenty of water

How to get there: 🚐 to Mancha Blanca (La Santa bus, Timetable 11)
To return: 🚐 from Tinajo (Timetable 11) or 🚕 taxi

Short walk: Mancha Blanca — Tinajo (6.5km/4mi; 1h45min). Easy stroll on country lanes, through beautiful farming country. Access/ return as above; wear comfortable shoes and take a sunhat. Follow the main walk for 55min, then fork right for Tinajo, picking up the main walk again at the 4h30min-point. If travelling by 🚕, park at Tinajo and take a bus to Mancha Blanca to start, picking up your car at the end of the walk.

This walk will not appeal to everyone. It takes you straight through the vast lava flows that have buried much of the southwest of Lanzarote. Not a soul lives out here — not even plants survive. It's a no-man's land. Deep in its midst, you stumble upon islands of lava-free ground, called *islotes* (see overleaf). Here you'll find some plant life and cultivation taking refuge. It's a curious landscape that few would dare to call beautiful, but it has a special allure.

Alight from your bus in **Mancha Blanca**, and **set off** by turning left towards the MASTS on the volcano just north of the village. Pass the SPORTS GROUND on the left and then turn left on the LZ67 road signposted to Timanfaya. Ignore all side-streets. You skirt this well-

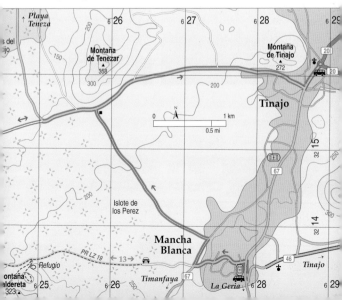

dispersed rural village. Stone walls hedge in the road and cordon off the countryside. Here you're on the edge of a sea of 'AA' lava (a sharp, unevenly-surfaced lava; photograph page 120). The grand crater dominating the scene is **Montaña Blanca** (Walk 13; see overleaf), and pint-sized **Montaña Caldereta** sits in front of it.

Just outside the village, 100m/yds past the last house, turn right on a tarred lane (**15min**). *(Walk 13 goes straight ahead here, on a track with PR LZ 19 signposting.)* From here you follow tarred country lanes through fields. Seven minutes later, before a solitary house ahead to the right, turn sharp left (by a 40KM SPEED RESTRICTION SIGN). Ignore all side-tracks. The sharp colour contrast of vivid green plots and ash-grey *lapilli* enhances this picturesque countryside. **Montaña de Tenezar** rises up boldly at the end of the road. Another junction awaits you at the foot of the mountain, where there is a SOLITARY FARM ahead

Left, top: curious 'islands' of greenery (chiefly tabaiba*) rise out of the lava. These islotes are patches of ground untouched by the eruptions in the 1700s. Tabaiba (left, middle) flourishes on the island, but* uvilla *(below) is confined to coastal areas. Bottom: waves crash on the Timanfaya coast ahead, as you near the Playa de la Madera.*

on the right (**55min**). Turn left (*right* for the Short walk). After passing two forks to the right (the first chained off), the tar peters out into a motorable track. You head into lava that now takes over the landscape. The craters of Montaña Blanca and son soon bulge up out of the lava. Up close, the mountain's rocky exterior resembles a freshly-baked cake.

Slowly, the off-shore islands appear: Alegranza, the furthest afield, Montaña Clara, and finally La Graciosa. The dark lava drops off into a deep blue sea. Without warning, suddenly the lava flow subsides and reveals a basin of low stony hillocks that lean up against Montaña Blanca like cushions. A couple of stone *casitas* can be seen, set in a coomb in the shoulders of the crater. This is Casas del Islote. You pass a fork off left to **Casas del Islote** and the Montañas del Fuego at about **1h45min** and dip down into an *islote*.

Some 25 minutes further on pass another turn-off to the right. From a rise eight minutes further on, you spot the first of the beaches, **Playa de las Malvas**. These black sand beaches are small and the waters usually turbulent. A tiny lagoon sits back off the beach here. Beyond this playa you head back into the lava again and, less than 15 minutes later, you drop down onto **Playa de la Madera** (**2h35min**). This small cove doesn't look too friendly either. Play it safe and stick to the rock pools. Pillows of yellow-tipped *Zygophyllum fontanesii* (*uvilla* — 'little grapes') grow out of the sand. A path crosses the beach and climbs into the rock on the other side, from where Walk 30 heads south. Shallow and inviting rock pools (only safe when the sea is calm) lie nearby.

Some 1h55min into the straightforward return walk you rejoin the road by the solitary farm below Montaña de Tenezar. This time, keep straight on for Tinajo. La Graciosa is at last in full view, and the Risco de Famara (Walk 2) dramatises the landscape as it bursts straight up out of the sea. **Tinajo** is a sprinkling of hamlets that sprawls over a large cultivated plain. Entering the village, keep straight along, passing all turn-offs to the right. On reaching a large intersection, go left, taking the second of the two roads leading down to the PLAZA (**5h20min**). The bus stop for Arrecife is in front of the church.

Walk 13: CALDERA BLANCA

See also photograph on page 4

Distance: 10km/6.2mi; 3h15min (13km/8mi; 4h if travelling by bus)

Grade: moderate, with an ascent of about 250m/820ft; possibility of vertigo on the crater rim (not recommended on windy days!). The loose stones underfoot on the path in the *malpais* make for tiring walking.

Equipment: walking boots (ankle-twisting terrain underfoot), fleece, sunhat, raingear, suncream, picnic, plenty of water

How to get there and return: 🚗 or 🚐 to/from Mancha Blanca (La Santa bus, Timetable 11). Travelling by 🚗, take the dirt track heading west off the LZ67 Timanfaya road just past the last houses of Mancha Blanca (the 41km-point on Car tour 2), by an information board. (Approaching from the south, this track is 1.5km north of the Timanfaya Visitors' Centre.) After 700m the track ends at a small car park. Travelling by 🚐, see Walk 12 (pages 77-78), to walk to the dirt track with the PR LZ 19 fingerposts and information board (add 1.5km each way).

Short walk: Montaña Caldereta (4km/2.5mi; 1h20min). No problems with vertigo, so easy — but tiring walking nevertheless. Follow the main walk to the *refugio* and return the same way.

The Municipality of Tinajo boasts that 65% of its terrain is under protection — not surprising, since it includes La Geria and the Timanfaya National Park! This walk is just outside the national park, but (like Walk 6) the Caldera Blanca area has become a protected UNESCO Geopark — the Los Volcanes Natural Park.

Start the walk at the PARKING AREA: in the company of the PR LZ 19, head due west on the clear path through the 'badlands' of AA lava. In just **10min** you're dipping into a depression in the *malpais* and arrive at the first Geopark INFORMATION BOARD explaining lava rivers. About a dozen more of these displays follow — sure to whet your interest in vulcanology.

At about **30min** into the walk you spot some smooth red soil and greenery ahead — a welcome respite from the veritable ocean of sharp rock through which you've been floundering. In fact there is a clear 'edge' to the lava: the flow stopped dead in its tracks here. Like the other volcanoes in this chain, **Montaña Caldereta**, on your left, is part of an *islote*, terrain untouched by the eruptions of the 1700s. Fork up left past a WELL to the ancient HUT (*refugio*; **40min**; Picnic 13). Take a break to admire the fertile basin and, if you hanker to walk *inside* a crater, this is a good place to do so; Montaña Blanca's is very steep!

Although cairns lead from here to Montaña Blanca, it's easy to go back to the main path and follow it west for 450m/yds, to where an ARROW OF LARGE STONES on the ground point you up a rough path via TWO CORRALS. Follow everyone else through a zigzag, up to the lowest point of **Montaña Blanca**'s CRATER RIM (**1h15min**).

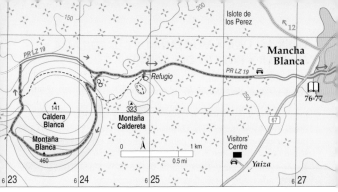

Now it's a steep 30 minute ascent to the SUMMIT TRIG POINT (**1h45min**), with its fantastic views into the perfectly circular basin and across the national park.

Descend the skiddy goats' path *carefully* until you reach a SADDLE (**2h15min**), from where the walking is a bit easier. Descend to the track seen below, and turn right. Just past a PR LZ 19 FINGERPOST you regain your outward path. Follow it back to the CAR PARK (**3h15min**).

Clockwise from right: the red-earth Caldereta islote is a most welcome sight in the sea of lava; it's an easy descent to the crater floor, but it's impressive nonetheless; walkers on the saddle: some will descend left into the crater, others start on the path to the right, to Caldera Blanca; the ancient stone stone hut (refugio) with its wattle-and-daub walls has an oven

Walk 14: UGA • MONTAÑA DE GUARDILAMA • MACHER • PUERTO DEL CARMEN

Distance: 12.5km/7.8mi; 3h40min

Grade: relatively easy climb of 200m/650ft and descent of 420m/1375ft, *excluding* the ascent of Guardilama. The ascent of Guardilama involves an additional steep climb and descent of 180m/590ft, sometimes over loose stones. The climb is also to be avoided in hot weather, but remember, on the other hand, that the peak can be very cold and windy! *Note:* this route is sometimes followed by jeep safaris.

Equipment: walking shoes (boots if ascending Guardilama), jacket, sunhat, suncream, raingear, picnic, plenty of water

How to get there: 🚌 to Uga (Playa Blanca bus, Timetable 5). Travelling by 🚗, you could leave your car in Puerto del Carmen and take one of the frequent buses into Arrecife for the connecting bus to Uga.
To return: 🚌 from Puerto del Carmen (Timetables 2, 12), or your 🚗

The island's farming methods are of much interest on Lanzarote. With great ingenuity the islanders have been able to grow a variety of produce. This hike, partly along the GR131 and then the PR LZ 06, takes you through the dark ash fields of La Geria — an intriguing landscape patterned by hollows and stone walls. You then cross the grassy summits that divide east and west, two quite different worlds! The *mirador* atop Montaña de Guardilama reveals a world of vivid contrasts: vineyards and vegetable plots, meadows and ash fields, and the great lava flows. It opens up the interior of the island for you, and you have a fine outlook over the lunar landscape of the Timanfaya National Park.

Leave the bus at the cheerful square in **Uga**. **Start out** with your back to the CHURCH door: head left (back the way the bus came in). Pass a GAMES COURT on the left and

From the top of Guardilama, you have a superb view over the Geria Valley and to the mountains of Timanfaya.

walk past Calle El Ganchillo on your right. Keep straight on to a junction, where you first fork left and then immediately right on a wide road. Some 150m/yds before the main LZ30 to La Geria and Teguise, turn left on CALLE LOS ARENALES. Two minutes along, leave the road and climb a farm track on the right, the first one you come to. The route overlooks the village, which nestles in a shallow depression of gardens, its back to a vast expanse of crusty lava. Out of the lava rise the great fire mountains of Timanfaya, their inclines splashed with rust browns and reds. A cluster of hills stands to the south of the village. These climb into the southern massif — Los Ajaches.

The track carries you up to the TEGUISE ROAD, where you turn left. A few minutes along (50m/yds past the KM22 STONE), fork right onto another track bristling with walkers' and mountain bikers' FINGERPOSTS. You're now entering the **Geria Valley**. Vines and fig trees fill the small hollows. The ash fields are ornamented by an assortment of stone walls. Your route will take you straight over the *cumbre*, the island's spine. Ignore all turn-offs. Wandering through this blackened world is quite extraordinary. Over to the left, the lava fields grow into a vast lake ruptured by weather-worn cones, and above you stands a line of grass-capped hills that glow with greenery. The solitary white farmsteads stand out like sanctuaries in this inhospitable landscape. Before long, walls take over the countryside. You're entering the vineyards, and the inclines are pock-marked with depressions that are collared by half-circles of stone walls (see pages 28-29 and opposite). You're in malmsey territory, where the well-known *malvasía* originates. This myriad of walls could be the ruins of a grand ancient city.

Crossing the saddle of the *cumbre* the way eases out. You'll have a superb view back over La Geria and Timanfaya (Picnic 14). At the top of the PASS (**1h**), a track turns off right to a paragliders' launching site. (*Walk 15 goes right here.*) Just beyond this turning, head left up a path/track through the vines for the ascent of Montaña Guardilama. When the track ends, continue straight up to the summit — a tiring climb, as it's very steep.

At the **1h30min**-mark you flop down on the SUMMIT of **Montaña de Guardilama**. If it's a windy day, you won't be able to stand upright or even take photos up here! The panorama is, however, magnificent and encompasses the waves of hills in the south, as well as the Risco de Famara and La Graciosa and its neighbouring islets in

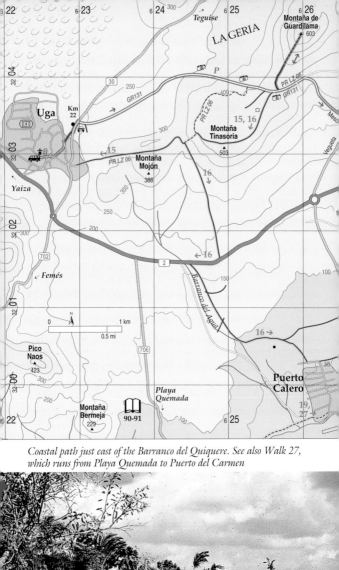

Coastal path just east of the Barranco del Quiquere. See also Walk 27, which runs from Playa Quemada to Puerto del Carmen

the north. The sharp, rocky mountain crest drops straight down into a cultivated crater and out onto the pitted ash fields of La Geria. Uga and Yaiza (Walk 17) lie to the southeast.

Descend slowly and carefully to the main track (**2h**), and head left towards La Asomada. Ignore a track to the right but, 100m/yds further on, leave the main track at a Y-fork: descend another motorable track to the right (CAMINO DEL MESON), which shortly acquires a tarmac surface. You drop down through plots, in 15 minutes crossing the road to La Asomada. At the next intersection turn left on the tarmac lane (CAMINO SAN PEDRO). At the following junction, after 300m/yds, turn right down to a T-junction (CAMINO LOS OLIVOS; **2h30min**).

Turn left, but after just 50m turn right and after only another 20m (just past a house with 'Geria'-style half-moon walls in its garden) cut right down a rough narrow track/path to the LZ2 seen below. Cross this speedway *carefully,* and pick up the track directly opposite (CAMINO LA CALDERINA). The track shortly becomes tarred and edged with garlands of pink and red geraniums as it passes the FINCA MACHINIDA on the left. The tar runs out before the next, Y-fork, where you go right, leaving a rougher track off to the left (a short-cut, but it may be private property). At the T-junction at the bottom of the track, turn left (CAMINO DEL PUERTO). About eight minutes later, just after rounding a bend, turn right on a tarred road. Ignore the Camino del Rompimiento to the right.

Turn right just before the main road on CAMINO BAR-

RANCO DEL QUIQUERE, another motorable track. While the views are limited, it's preferable to the main road *and* will give you the chance to follow a pretty stretch of coast. Cross straight over the road to Puerto Calero on CAMINO DEL POZO. After 50m/yds keep left at a junction. The track ends 500m/yds further on, at villas 13 and 15 (**3h15min**). Pass between the large boulders on the right, to join a footpath running along the eastern side of the **Barranco del Quiquere**. Walking below the colourful gardens shown on page 84 and then above a lido, follow the good coastal path 1.5km into **Puerto del Carmen** (**3h40min**).

The steep ascent of Guardilama

Walk 15: UGA • MONTAÑA TINASORIA • UGA

See photographs opposite and on page 82

Distance: 7.8km/4.8mi; 2h10min

Grade: moderate; ascent/descent of 280m/920ft overall, *excluding* the ascent of Guardilama (see Walk 14 if you plan to make that ascent).

Equipment: walking shoes (boots if ascending Guardilama), jacket, sunhat, suncream, raingear, picnic, plenty of water

How to get there and return: 🚗 (park near the church) or 🚌 to/from Uga (Playa Blanca bus, Timetable 5).

This entire walks takes place in La Geria, a perfect example of how man's need to tame nature for agricultural purposes results in the creation of a stunning landscape. The many thousands of half-moon drystone walls *(zocos)* of La Geria are dizzyingly beautiful.

Start out by following WALK 14 as far as the PASS (**1h**), just before the Guardilama ascent . Turn right here on a wide track through vineyards, and head straight up the hill past the PARAGLIDERS LAUNCH SITE and the large RUIN. You'll spot what looks like an old stone wall some 10m/yds to your right — in fact an old AQUEDUCT.

The track rises over the top of **Montaña Tinasoria** (503m; **1h20min**), and a fantastic view unfolds over the southeast coast, with Lobos and Fuerteventura in the distance. When the track peters out ahead, go straight into a steep, gravelly descent. Then, where the PR LZ 06 (Mozaga to Yaiza trail) veers off right to round Tinasoria's rim, make your way over to the left — towards some larger rocks on the side of the mountain (facing Uga and Yaiza). From the left of these rocks a steep and narrow (but not difficult) path zigzags down, and in just 10 minutes you reach the tracks below (**1h45min**).

Go straight on, walking right through the middle of **Montaña Mojón**. Coming out of this crater, ignore a path off right to a 'baby' crater. Soon the track becomes tarred; then you cross the LZ30 road and make your way back to the CHURCH SQUARE in **Uga** (**2h10min**).

Walk 16: UGA • MONTAÑA TINASORIA • PUERTO CALERO (OR PUERTO DEL CARMEN)

See photographs on pages 82, 84, 86
Distance: 12.5km/7.8mi; 3h *to Puerto Calero* (4h to Puerto del Carmen)
Grade: moderate, with an ascent of 280m/920ft and descent of 500m/1640ft. *Note:* this route is sometimes followed by jeep safaris.
Equipment/Access: as Walk 14, page 82

What could be more enjoyable than a countryside hike through the half-moon vineyards of La Geria, working up an appetite, followed by a gentle descent to the coast and an alfresco seaside lunch?

Start out by following WALK 15 TO THE 1H45MIN-POINT. Instead of heading into the Mojón crater, turn left and descend a track straight downhill. After 20 minutes you meet the LZ2 (**2h05min**); follow it to the right for 400m/yds, then cross *carefully* and take a downhill track opposite, crossing straight over two junctions (**2h10min, 2h15min**). As you pass a small *barranco* on your right, the track veers slightly left. At a fork just past a FARM with old drystone buildings, keep right (**2h25min**).

Meeting a tarred road in a few minutes, turn left and walk down to the MARINA at **Puerto Calero** (**3h**). You can pick up a bus at the roundabout on the Puerto del Carmen road or head east and follow the coastal path/track on to **Puerto del Carmen** (Walk 27; **4h**).

Walk 17: YAIZA • ATALAYA DE FEMÉS • YAIZA

See also photographs pages 97 and 101

Distance: 10km/6.2mi; 4h

Grade: fairly strenuous, with a steady 425m/1435ft ascent. Can be cold and windy.

Equipment: comfortable walking shoes, jacket, sunhat, raingear, suncream, picnic, plenty of water

How to get there and return: 🚐 to/from Yaiza (Playa Blanca bus, Timetable 5), or 🚗

Short walk: Femés — Atalaya de Femés — Femés (3.2km/2mi; 1h 30min; a strenuous, but short, ascent/descent of 300m/1000ft). Equipment as above; access/return by 🚐 (Timetable 4, but scheduling is currently inconvenient) or 🚗 to/from Femés. Facing the Bar Femés, walk up the road at its left-hand side, keeping the church on your left. You will meet a brick-paved road: follow it uphill to the right. At the top of the road, where it bends right to rejoin the main road, take the concrete track up to the left (just in front of a green garage door). At the next junction, go straight ahead on an asphalted road. After 50m/yds this becomes a dirt track: follow it for 300m/yds, then turn left up a chained-off track.

Alternative walks

1 **Femés — Atalaya de Femés — Yaiza** (7.5km/4.7mi; 2h30min). Fairly strenuous, with an initial ascent of 300m/1000ft; the rest of the way is downhill. Access: 🚐 (Timetable 4) or 🚗 taxi to Femés; return by 🚐 from Yaiza (Timetable 5). Follow the Short walk (above) to the Atalaya de Femés, then use the map on page 88 to descend to Yaiza.

2 **Yaiza — Atalaya de Femés — Femés** (7.5km/4.7mi; 3h30min). Grade, access, equipment as main walk. Follow the main walk to the Atalaya (2h30min), then go back down to the junction with your outgoing path and follow the track down to the right. Follow the main track until you reach the chain and, 20m/ yds further down, turn right. When you meet asphalt, go over an intersection. At the next crossing, go right, then left. Follow the brick-paved road to the square at Femés. Walks 18 and 19 start here, affording many possibilities for the fighting fit — on cooler, cloudy days!

Picnic 17: view down over Femés on the climb to the Atalaya

The view from the Atalaya de Femés is best appreciated at sunrise and sunset, when shadows creep across the countryside, and the last (or first) light captures the real beauty of both Timanfaya and the Salinas de Janubio. Sitting high above the picturesque hamlet of Femés, you have the southern vista of Lanzarote all to yourself. On your ascent you'll often see camels grazing in one of the adjoining valleys. Nearer the summit, goats and a few sheep keep you company.

The bus drops you just before the SQUARE in **Yaiza**. This bleached-white village has won a number of awards for its appearance. It really is picture postcard-perfect, with its resplendent bougainvillea and graceful palms. **Start off** by taking the ROAD TO LA DEGOLLADA: it heads uphill between the CHURCH and the square, to a large parking area with a restaurant. Continue uphill, past a huge PLAZA on the left and a beautiful PARK on the right (built to commemorate the the 250th anniversary of the Timanfaya eruptions). Turn left on a wide street beyond the plaza (about 50m/yds *before* the walled-in CEMETERY, which can be seen ahead on the left-hand side of the road). Cutting across the valley floor, you look up into a tapering valley and see the hamlet of La Degollada ensconced at the end of it. Your ongoing track is visible ahead. When the tarmac ends at an intersection, go straight ahead on a cinder track. Ascending the valley wall, pass a faint fork off to the left. Mount the crest just over **20min** from Yaiza, by a RUINED WINDMILL on the left. A track coming up from Uga joins from the left; you continue up this plump ridge, which will carry you all the way to the Atalaya de Femés.

As you climb, the island opens up, revealing a variety of scenery. Yaiza is in full view below, its brightness accentuated by the intense green garden plots and the dark sea of lava. A barrier of volcanoes, one running into the next, fills in the back-drop. About 1km along this wide track, just beyond the brow of the hill, take a right

Casa de Cultura at Yaiza, opposite the church, in the main square

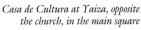

turn marked by CAIRNS, going through a gap in the wall. Your view becomes more expansive and more rewarding — dipping down now onto Uga and stretching all the way up the dark, shadowy Geria Valley (Walks 14-16). Some 200m/yds past the turn-off, at a fork, keep right. Mounting another step in the ridge, you see over the sloping plains of the east to Puerto del Carmen and Arrecife. Looking north, notice the line of three lopsided craters. The way dips briefly before reascending, and you enjoy an introductory glimpse of the Femés valley. Montaña de Timanfaya, the king of the volcanoes, dominates the national park, with its distinct reddish-brown slopes.

The way fades as it remounts the top of the crest, which in turn narrows into a sheer-sided 'neck'. Another striking sight follows: the off-white salt pans and the khaki-green lagoon of the Salinas del Janubio shimmering in the sun. Eventually the path meets the Atalaya de Femés track (**2h15min**). Head right, up to the SUMMIT of the **Atalaya de Femés** (608m/1995ft; **2h30min**). A stupendous view unfolds. The remote (for this island!) little village of Femés lies straight below, huddled around the pass that descends to the Rubicón plain. Fuerteventura and Lobos fill in the backdrop. And from up here you can almost count the colourful volcanoes of Timanfaya. On the far side of the transmitter station, you look down onto Las Breñas, stretching along a raised shelf of cultivation that steps off onto the Rubicón.

From the top, allow 1h30min to return to **Yaiza** (**4h**). The BUS STOP is at the zebra crossing north of the plaza.

Walk 18: THREE *BARRANCOS:* A CIRCUIT FROM FEMES

See also photographs pages 101 and 102

Distance: 7.5km/4.7mi; 2h40min

Grade: moderate climbs and descents of about 320m/1050ft overall, but you must be sure-footed and have a head for heights (possibility of vertigo on one stretch). There is also volcanic rubble underfoot for much of the walk — good ankle support is needed. The last part of the walk is a fairly steep ascent of 180m/600ft in full sun— quite a slog.

Equipment: stout shoes with good ankle support (or walking boots), warm jacket, sunhat, raingear, suncream, picnic, plenty of water

How to get there and return: 🚌 (Timetable 4) or 🚗 to/from Femés. The bus shelter is by a supermarket: when you alight, walk 200m/yds towards Playa Blanca to reach the roundabout where the walk begins.

Short walk: Femés — Degollada del Portugués — Femés (3.5km/2.2mi; 1h35min). Equipment and access as main walk. Climb and descent of only 100m/330ft, but there is a possibility of vertigo on one short stretch. Follow the main walk to the 50min-point and return the same way.

Alternative walk: Femés — Playa de Papagayo — Playa Blanca (20km/12.4mi; 5h15min). This is Walk 20 in reverse; equipment and access as above; return by 🚌 from Playa Blanca. Follow the main walk to the fork at the 45min-point and bear right. This path tends to fizzle out in goat tracks, but try to keep to the main zigzag path, or you'll have a terrible skid over the volcanic rubble. In less than five minutes you descend to another, smaller goat house. Ahead of you here is the dirt track followed in Walk 20. To continue to Papagayo (photograph page 14) and Playa Blanca, turn left on this track. Entire route is PR LZ 09.

This short circuit is one of my favourite walks on Lanzarote, and it's ideal for motorists. If you've energy to spare at the end, why not climb up to the Atalaya de Femés (Alternative walk 17-1) to watch the sunset?

Perhaps in part owing to the burgeoning of Playa Blanca as a resort, in recent years interest has grown enormously in walking in this southwestern corner of Lanzarote. The local council set up a 'Network of Ajaches Footpaths' *(Red de Senderos)*, and you may see some old information boards detailing the routes. We've shown many of their paths in this area on the map overleaf, most of which have been taken over by the island government *(cabildo)*. The map also shows the route of the well-signposted GR131 heading out of Playa Blanca as it crosses the island to Orzola in the north.

From the ROUNDABOUT on the main road in **Femés**, **start out** by following the PR LZ 09 fingerposts up the tarred lane opposite the bar, making for some ugly concrete buildings seen ahead on the hilltop. The tarmac peters out, and in **5min** you pass between two *aljibes* (water tanks set into the ground). Continue up to the buildings, and walk just to the right of the main building,

93

still on the road/track. Looking to the left now the reason for this blot on the landscape reveals itself: there's the amusing sight of a GOAT FARM, and the large pen may be bursting with these delightful creatures, which are bound to keep you company later in the walk. The buildings lie at the edge of a crest, the **Loma del Pico de la Aceituna** (414m/1358ft; **10min**). From here you look down over the isolated **Barranco de la Higuera** — a huge abyss, lime-green to gold in colour, due to the sparse sprinkling of grasses in the volcanic soil. Straight below you, the dry river bed traces an intricate meander in a wonderfully pristine landscape.

At this point you have a choice of two paths, as indicated on the INFORMATION BOARDS to the right. The PR LZ 10/11 heads left, straight down into the valley *(the route of the Walk 19, and the return route for the main walk)*. The other, the PR LZ 09, heads west round the head of the valley: look right and you'll spot it, cut into the ledge and accompanied by a black pipe. Walk towards it, passing to the left of another building (a water basin half sunken into the rock), and bearing slightly left downhill.

As you approach a saddle between **Pico de la Aceituna** and Pico Redondo, the way fades over bedrock, but small stones on either side of the path keep you in line. You curl up left to the SADDLE and at **30min** enjoy a superb view to Playa Blanca and Corralejo on Fuerteventura. The setting is always more photogenic on windy days, when scudding clouds create an ever-changing mosaic on the featureless Rubicón plain below. The little volcano to the west of Playa Blanca, Montaña Roja, is climbed in Walk 21; beyond it are the lighthouses at Pechiguera.

By **40min** a new *barranco* on your right drops away steeply to the hairpins of the jeep track that comes up to meet the track followed in the Alternative walk and Walk 20. Some people may find this stretch vertiginous, although the path is amply wide. Five minutes later (**45min**) be alert for a fork in the path. Your route is to the left. *(But the Alternative walk goes right here with the PR LZ 09.)* You climb the flanks of **Pico Redondo** for just two minutes, to reach a pass, the **Degollada del Portugués** (Picnic 18). You're above and to the left of the Papagayo track followed in the Alternative walk. Looking below, to the right, you'll spot the small goat farm shown on page 102; the Alternative walk passes it. A minute later there is a wonderful view east to Puerto

The pretty church square in Femés

Calero, Puerto del Carmen and the outskirts of Arrecife. A second deep *barranco,* the **Barranco de la Casita,** opens out in front of you here.

Leaving the pass (and keeping an eye out for zigzags in the path), soon a third gash opens up on the right — the **Barranco de los Dises.** On the far side is **Hacha Grande**; rusty volcanic hues ripple down its flanks. Ahead is a ROCKY KNOLL colonised by an incredible variety of plants — it stands out like a huge green *sombrero* in this hostile terrain. At **1h** you're passing just to the left of the 'hat' and walking an exhilarating RIDGE between the two *barrancos* — the Dises on your right and the Casita on your left. A solitary cairn can be spotted ahead ('302' on the map). The path bends to the left 80m/yds before this point is reached, however. Your ongoing path can be spotted on the far side of the Barranco de la Casita, making for a stone shelter.

Descend into the *barranco,* where you'll spot a good variety of wild flowers in spring, as well as the ubiquitous yellow-flowering *aulaga* ('canary firebush', see overleaf). The **1h20min**-mark sees you crossing the dry *barranco,* still making for the shelter ahead. The SHELTER (built in 1996; **1h30min**) is a lovely stone-built resting place with seats and welcome shade. Beside it another *aljibe* catches the rainwater off the slopes of Pico Redondo.

Go back to the U-turn in the path just before the shelter and head uphill towards the **Morro de la Loma del Pozo,** a ridge which can be seen ahead. The path becomes a track. As you gain height, the Atalaya de Femés comes into view once more. At **1h43min** pass a track off right to the top of the Morro (20min there and back). Two minutes later, the track veers right: continue left on the path. More stones line the route in this area, to keep you on course. From this angle, Pico Redondo is a smooth cone to the left.

By **1h50min** you're descending into the **Barranco de la Higuera** — the first *barranco* you saw from the goat house. On the far (eastern) side, the track to Playa Quemada (Walk 19) stands out clearly. If you've timed your walk right, the goats will now lead you back to

The meandering Barranco de la Higuera, looking east into the early-morning sun — a pristine landscape.

Aulaga (Lotus lancerottensis; *top*) *and various* Euphorbias *predominate in the valleys, along with* Nicotiana glauca *(the tobacco plant, second from top). But hidden in rock crevices you'll spot many other species struggling to survive, such as yellow cut-leaf* Reichardia tingitana *and purple-flowering bugloss* (Eichium lancerottense).

Femés. They'll come inquisitively (but timidly) trouping in from the slopes behind the Morro and make their way up to the farm 'for lunch' — just follow them up *(but later in the climb, when the paths narrow, please keep out of their way; they are **not** tame)*.

As you approach a PYLON, ruined stone walls and pens lining the path testify to a long history of goat-rearing in the valley. Just past the pylon, keep right on a narrow path and, 100m/yds further on, turn left. *(Walk 19 follows the path on the right here.)* This path runs between the walls and more ruined pens — following the electricity cables. The goat farm is visible up to the right. Pico de la Aceituna is to the left now; your outgoing path is etched into its flanks.

Soon you leave the electricity wires and cross a dry *barranco*, making for the goat farm. Many 'skiddy' goat paths thread the area; if there are no goats to guide you, just keep making for your destination on the best path — all paths lead to the goat farm! At **2h12min** a fairly steep dry *barranco* (offshoot of the Higuera) is crossed. Ahead, at the top of the valley, volcanic hues ooze out of the rock — burgundy, rust, cream, black. Ten minutes later, for the final assault, you can either zigzag up the main path or climb more or less straight up the bedrock near the edge of the *barranco*. Once you arrive back at the GOAT FARM (**2h30min**), descend to **Femés** (**2h 40min**).

Walk 19: Femés • Barranco de la Higuera • Playa Quemada • Puerto del Carmen

Map begins below and ends on pages 84-85; see also photographs pages 84, 89, 97, 98

Distance: 12km/7.4mi; 4h30min

Grade: a 10-minute climb at the outset, then a descent of 400m/1300ft (sometimes slippery underfoot), followed by some ups and downs over headlands. All PR LZ 11

Equipment: stout shoes with good ankle support (or walking boots), warm jacket, sunhat, raingear, suncream, picnic, swimwear, plenty of water

How to get there : 🚌 to Femés (Timetable 4)
To return: 🚌 from Puerto del Carmen (Timetables 2, 12)

Alternative walk: Playa Quemada — Barranco de la Higuera — Lomo del Pozo — Playa Quemada (10km/6.2mi; 4h10min). Moderate, with an ascent/descent of about 350m/1150ft; equipment as main walk. Access: 🚗 to/from Playa Quemada. Follow the coastal path to the Barranco de la Higuera (40min), where you should note your return path (PR LZ 11) coming in from the right. Continue on the coastal path until a purple waymark on the right signals an ascent up the Morro de la Loma del Pozo (1h15min). Eventually joining Walk 18 (2h), follow it down the Barranco de la Higuera and on to Playa Quemada (4h10min).

The 'Red de Senderos de los Ajaches' referred to on page 93 opened up a wealth of walks in this southwestern corner of Lanzarote; some of the routes, like this one, were 'upgraded' as PR walks by the island government.

Start out by following WALK 18 TO THE GOAT FARM (**10min**), then take the narrow PR LZ 11 path which heads left initially, then bends right and descends steeply into the **Barranco de la Higuera**. On the descent, looking left, you can see your ongoing route to the sea — an old washed-out track. About 100m/yds before an electricity pylon, ignore a path to the right (the return route for both Walk 18 *and* the Alternative walk). Zigzag down to the track and, once on it, ignore a track to the right which climbs the Morro de la Lomo del Pozo (approached from the south in the Alternative walk) and a footpath to the left.

Follow the left-hand side of the *barranco* down to a small beach if you want to swim; otherwise, a couple of hundred metres before the beach, cross a dry riverbed and follow it towards the sea, where the clear track off to the left (still the PR LZ 11) leads to Playa de la Arena and Playa Quemada. Almost at the top of the headland, on a bend, pick up the path again. It winds above the coastline with fabulous views of the blue, blue ocean. Five minutes later, ignore a path heading left inland, then another path down to Playa de la Arena. Reaching **Playa Quemada** (**2h30min**), use the notes on page 122 (Walk 27; see map on pages 84-85) to go on to **Puerto del Carmen** (**4h30min**).

The 'Balcón de Femés' overlooks the Rubicón plain and Playa Blanca. On the climb to the goat farm, you look back down on Femés and over to the Atalaya de Femés, setting for Walk 17 and Picnic 17.

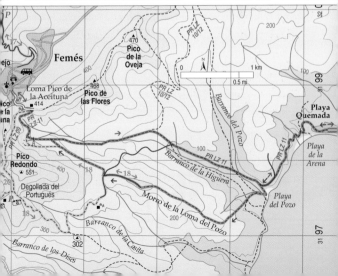

Walk 20: PLAYA BLANCA • PLAYA DE PAPAGAYO • BARRANCO PARRADO • FEMES

See map pages 94-95; see also photographs page 14, 97, 101

Distance: 20km/12.4mi; 6h

Grade: strenuous, with ascents of about 550m/1800ft overall — most of it at the end of the walk. There is no shade en route, and it can be very hot, so keep this walk for cool overcast days — or *do it in reverse* (see Alternative walk below). The entire route is PR LZ 09.

Equipment: comfortable walking shoes or walking boots, fleece, sunhat, suncream, raingear, picnic, plenty of water, swimwear

How to get there and return: 🚌 to Playa Blanca (Timetables 5, 12) and return from Femés (Timetable 4). Or 🚗 to/from Playa Blanca: on arrival, arrange with a taxi to collect you from Femés at the end of the walk (or telephone from one of the bars when you arrive at Femés).

Shorter walk: Playa Blanca — Playa de Papagayo — Playa Blanca (10km/6.2mi; 3h). Fairly easy, with ascents/descents of about 100m/300ft overall; equipment and access as above. You can make the walk even shorter (6km/3.7mi; 2h10min): take the half-hourly Playa Blanca town bus to the most easterly stop, Las Coloradas, or drive there. There are blue walkers' signs just east of the stop, opposite a shopping centre.

Alternative walk: See Alternative walk 18 on page 93 to do this walk in reverse, downhill from Femes. All signposted PR LZ 09.

Sooner or later you'll discover the island's most beautiful beaches — those east of Playa Blanca, of which Playa de Papagayo is the best known. All are accessible by track, but this walk meanders along the jutting coastline, dipping down into each of these delightful beaches, most of which cater unofficially for naturists. You can bet your boots they'll lure you back another day. With the last of the beaches behind you, you're unlikely to see another soul, save for a goatherd. The landscape is sliced up by ravines and hidden valleys, shut off from the rest of the island by a wall of high hills.

Start off by following the brick-paved COASTAL

Walks 18 and 20: near the Degollada del Portugués you overlook the winding track to Papagayo running below Lomo Blanco on the flanks of Hacha Grande.

PROMENADE east from **Playa Blanca**, walking towards the CIRCULAR TOWER on the headland. Keep to the walkway past the RUBICON MARINA and the eye-catching 'volcanic cone' of the HOTEL VOLCAN. You reach this well-restored tower (**Castillo de las Coloradas**, bearing the date 1769 and also called **Torre de Aguila**) in **30min**. Off this headland you have a good view back to Playa Blanca and towards the superb beaches scooped out of the open bay on your left which culminates in the Punta de Papagayo.

The wide promenade rises and falls as it curves along the coast past several large apartment and hotel complexes. Surprisingly, there is still some undeveloped land in this prime location. After crossing a BRIDGE, you come to **Playa de las Coloradas** (also called **Playa del Afe**). This stony beach is the ugly duckling of the *playas*. Just past the beach the promenade ends in front of the HOTEL PAPAGAYO ARENA, from where a steep and skiddy path leads up to the headland.* Once at the top, you find a clear path over to Playa Mujeres. Low spiny *aulaga* lies scattered across the plain. Wherever you find *aulaga* there's usually *cosco* nearby. *Cosco* (the red ice plant) turns a vivid wine colour under drought conditions, and great colonies of it stain the inclines. Its fruit was used to make a substitute *gofio* (normally a roasted corn flour), and was used as a thickening agent in soups, etc.

Some **1h05min** into the walk the unspoilt **Playa Mujeres** is in sight. This lovely open beach stretches across the mouth of a shallow *barranco*. El Papagayo, the only sign of civilisation out here, is the handful of buildings near the point. Your path drops down into a small gravelly *barranco* and mounts a faint track which leads you down onto the golden sandy beach. You look back into the windswept hills of Los Ajaches. Near the end of the beach, scale the sandy bank to remount the crest — a steep, slippery three-minute climb on sand, followed by loose gravel. Continuing along the top of the crest, you dip in and out of small *barrancos* which empty out into concealed coves below.

Playa del Pozo is the next of the larger beaches. You can either clamber down a narrow stream bed to reach it,

*This path is the 'traditional' route: everybody uses it. But if you don't fancy the scramble, walk back 400m/yds and turn right just before the bridge, heading for the signposted commercial centre. Pass a parking area and, 150m/yds from the seafront, bear right. Pick up a path between the commercial centre to the right and gardens to the left. A blue walkers' sign indicates 'Playas de Papagayo' from here. In a couple of minutes an information board signals the the new 'official' trail to the headland.

or follow the trail straight on down along the ridge
(easier). Ascend the goats' path that edges around the
hillside at the end of the beach, and once again you're
above the sea. If the way appears vertiginous, scramble
up onto the plain straight up from the beach. Now more
enticing coves reveal themselves. Most days you'll find
they're occupied. Soon the old settlement of Papagayo
reappears on the crest of the ridge ahead. Circling behind
a couple of coves you reach the top of the crest and come
to **El Papagayo** (**1h45min**); there are three bar/restau-
rants here, if you're in need of refreshment. A rust-brown
and deep mauve-coloured rocky promontory separates
the two dazzling coves on either side of you. From here
you have a striking view of the smooth-faced inland hills,
as well as along the string of beaches you've just visited
(see photograph page 14). If you're only doing the Short
walk, you'll have plenty of time to sample these paradisial
beaches and coves (Picnic 20); otherwise, you'll only have
time for a couple of them.

Continuing on, follow the path curving around the
walls of **Playa de Papagayo**. Ice-plants and *cosco* patch the
slope. (If this path looks unnerving, make your way
around via the top of the crest.) Shortly meet a track
coming in from your left and follow it out to **Punta de
Papagayo**. It passes a pillbox a couple of minutes along
and then swings sharply back left. The point is just beyond
the shelter. Don't go too near to the edge of the cliffs on
windy days! Fuerteventura is now closer than ever, and
the dark 'pimply' island of Lobos is made more prominent
by the sand dunes of Corralejo in the background. Back
to your left you can see Puerto del Carmen and Arrecife
— a vast expanse of white trimming the sloping sea-plain.
A staggered chain of cone-shaped hills runs down the
centre of the island.

A few minutes below the PILLBOX (at about **2h**) the
track fizzles out onto yet another beach — **Caleta del
Congrio**, with its large camp site. Five minutes along the
beach (trying not to look left or right), reach the car park.
Follow the track north to the next cove, a minute over,
and then ascend to the top of the cliffs beyond it. Bits and
pieces of track lead you along these cliffs. Some 15
minutes from the last beach you come onto a clearer track
and overlook a rocky cove set at the mouth of a deep
ravine. Here you turn up left, keeping straight up (bear
left at the fork you encounter and go through an intersection), until you meet a T-junction (at about **2h45min**).

Turning right at the junction, you now sidle along the hills, disappearing further out 'into the sticks'. No more beaches, no more people ... but perhaps a goatherd and a handful of goats. Ignoring all tracks left and right, you ascend very gradually while looking straight off the sloping shelf onto the sea. The way curves back into a number of *barrancos* that slice inland. Some **3h30min** en route, drop down into a good-sized gully and cross a wide gravelly stream bed. The countryside can be surprisingly green out here in winter and spring. Still no sign of life, nor any trees ... a desolate spot indeed.

Tías comes into full view, its elevated slopes speckled with white buildings. The surrounding hills have subsided into a gentle rolling landscape. A brief descent takes you down to another *barranco* crossing. Now the hard work begins — a climb of over 400m/1300ft lies ahead. You wind your way up into the largest of the valleys so far encountered, the **Barranco Parrado**. Dandelions and *Echium* add their golds and purples to the greenery if you walk in spring. Some seven-eight minutes uphill from the stream bed crossing, come to an junction and head left. Several minutes later, you'll see a shepherds' crumbled outpost on a rocky outcrop above the track. On a windy day it's a good picnic shelter. There's also a large colony of ice plants here. This plant was once traded for its soda content. Pico Redondo (551m/1800ft; Walk 18) is the peak rising over on your right, between the Casita and Higuera *barrancos*. Soon you encounter the first trees — some rather scrawny examples of *Solanaceae* (the tomato family) — scattered along the side of the track.

A fantastic viewpoint (where you're often hit by a gale-force wind), awaits you when you reach a pass below the Degollada del Portugués (**5h**). A small GOAT FARM sits nearby. Make your way to it, then climb the slippery slope behind it (there *is* a zigzag path here, but a myriad of goats' trails have nearly obliterated it). In five minutes you'll come to a fork on the **Degollada del Portugués**, but you may not notice it. The path heading sharply back to the right is the route of Walk 18. Keep straight on, with a steep *barranco* hard on your left, as you round the flanks of **Pico Redondo**. By **5h50min** you'll stagger up to a LARGE GOAT FARM — a great photo opportunity! Turn down left on a track before the largest of the buildings: **Femés** is just ten minutes below (**6h**). Collapse in the bar at the 'Balcón de Femés', overlooking the Rubicón plain, while you wait for your transport.

Walk 21: MONTAÑA ROJA

See also town plan pages 8-9   **Distance:** 3km/2mi; 1h05min

Grade: an easy climb/descent of 130m/425ft, but the volcanic pumice underfoot is slippery. An ideal walk for those with children. No shade.

Equipment: comfortable walking shoes with ankle support, fleece, sunhat, suncream, water

How to get there and return: 🚗 to the roundabout outside Playa Blanca, then take the road for 'Faro de Pechiguera'. Pass the Corbeta Hotel on the left after about 1km, go straight over the next roundabout and, at the next (third) roundabout, turn right for Jardines del Sol (among others). Pass Los Claveles on the left, then keep ahead following the sign 'To the Volcano'. Park around here in one of the streets below the easily-seen path up the crater. Or: 🚌 (Timetables 5, 12) to the bus station in Playa Blanca, then town 🚐 30 (see box on page 9) to Virginia Park. Sometimes the names are missing from the bus stops: Virginia Park is the second stop after Colegio. From the stop walk seaward, then take the first right (Calle de Noruega), passing Los Claveles on the left.

Whether you're staying at Playa Blanca or just driving through, here's a short leg-stretcher to start or end your day. Montaña Roja is just a little pimple of a volcano, but in spring wonderful miniature gardens of wild flowers flourish in the pumice and, as the mountain rises in isolation on the Rubicón plain, you have far-reaching views.

Start out at the 'TO THE VOLCANO' sign: follow the street uphill to access the path. It's only **15min** up to the rim, where you can go either left or right. (For Picnic 21, you might like to turn left and reach the trig point in 10 minutes.) Heading right, you soon passing a path into

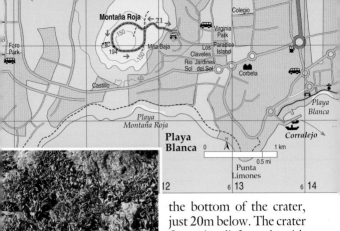

the bottom of the crater, just 20m below. The crater floor is disfigured with 'graffiti' — small stones arranged to spell out the names of previous visitors. As you round the basin, the urban sprawl and a network of roads comes into view — one leading to the large Atlante del Sol ruin in the northwest, a landmark on Walk 22. It stands isolated in a desert wilderness.

In about **45min** or a little more you will reach the **Montaña Roja** TRIG POINT, the highest point of the walk (194m). From here there's a fine view down to the lighthouses at Pechiguera and over to the dunes in the north of Fuerteventura. You'll be back at the junction in another 10 minutes and down at the 'VOLCANO' SIGN in **1h05min**.

Rounding Montaña Roja's small crater, you look down over an urban sprawl to the lighthouses at Punta de Pechiguera. In the immediate surroundings are 'rock gardens', where plants like leaf-lichen (Ramalina bourgeana; top) and fagiona (Fagiona cretica; bottom) flourish.

Distance: 11km/6.8mi; 3h45min

Grade: moderate; the terrain is mostly level underfoot, but you're floundering over uneven lava for much of the way. The final descent to El Convento is vertiginous and dangerous if wet (but this may be omitted). *No shade.*

Equipment: stout shoes with grip or walking boots, sunhat, suncream, fleece, raingear, picnic, plenty of water, swimwear

How to get there and return: 🚌 to/from La Hoya (Playa Blanca bus, Timetable 5). If you are travelling by 🚗, there are several places to park (see map). The best choices are the large *mirador* on the south side of the Salinas de Janubio or behind the water desalination plant — a large isolated dark yellow building off the LZ701 (old road), 2.4km south of the El Golfo roundabout, and start and end the walk there.

If you're tired of picnicking at the beach and eating sandwiches 'à la grit', then this coastal walk, with its superb unvisited rock pools, may be just what you're looking for. Beyond Playa de Janubio you follow a jagged, rocky coastline. There are no more beaches (or people), only natural rock pools — pools to suit all the family — hidden on the lava shelves that jut out into the sea. El Convento is the name given to the impressive sea cave at the end of the walk. It's a beautiful stretch of coastline, only frequented by the local fishermen.

Leave the bus at **La Hoya** (the junction for Las Breñas and El Golfo) and **start the walk:** follow the LZ701 south towards Playa Blanca, crossing straight over the roundabout. Less than **10min** along, just past the guard-rail, turn right. Walk over to a viewpoint that hangs out over the new salt pans on the right and the old, unused salt pans and lagoon facing the ocean. From here you have a bird's-eye view over the multitude of tiny white squares of salt and the evaporation ponds that divide up the basin floor, leaving it with a sunset-pink glow. The dark green lagoon enhances this fine setting, shown on page 112. This particular *salina* produces one-third of Lanzarote's salt. Ornithologists will be happy to know that this is a popular destination for migratory birds as well, and you can expect to find: teal, the cattle egret and little egret (on rare occasions); the grey heron and storks (from time to time); plovers, lapwing, and sparrow hawks (more commonly). Notice also the few derelict windmills down in the basin; these were used for pumping the seawater into the ponds.

The top of the plateau is bare and dusty. From above the lagoon continue south, circling the top of the basin. When you come to a small but deep RAVINE (a few minutes from the viewpoint, below the second round tower-like structure), clamber down the steep rocky face at its mouth. Take care, it's gravelly. A short descent drops you down onto the BASIN FLOOR, south of the lagoon. Follow the track over to your left to leave the basin. You'll pass by a shed and below a derelict house. Come onto the beach track at **30min**. **Playa de Janubio** sweeps around the shoreline below you. From here head south (left) along the edge of the sea plain, following trails the fishermen use.

Your continuation is a very faint track that lies across the beach track. It begins a minute uphill to your left. Keep close to the sea, so that you don't miss any of those alluring *charcos* (pools) and, where possible, scale down over the rock to check them out. You'll soon discover one that will steal an hour or two of your time. Your own private pool, too!

Along modest cliffs, you follow paths (sometimes marked by cairns) or just plough over the loose lava, and

On the outgoing leg, you follow paths the fishermen use, floundering over rough lava, so as not to miss any of the alluring rock pools. The return, on earthen tracks just inland from the coast, is far easier on the feet.

Above: rock pools (charcos) lie all along the route, and make delightful swimming holes, many of them suitable for children.

now and then you join up with a stretch of track. If you tire of floundering over all this rocky terrain, head inland for a couple of minutes and follow the main track (the return route), keeping parallel with the coast. Soon you're looking straight across the stone-strewn Rubicón plain to the pointed Ajache hills. In the distance, further along the coast, the water desalination plant and the abandoned *urbanización* of Atlante del Sol with its ugly ruin bare themselves. Las Breñas is the village you soon see strung out along the edge of an elevated plateau that steps back off the Rubicón. The landscape is still and lifeless, without a drop of colour.

In under **1h** you walk behind the WATER DESALINATION PLANT. Stretches of the coastal lava resemble cobblestone paving.

The Salinas de Janubio, where the walk starts and ends.

About 10-15 minutes beyond the water plant you begin finding the best pools (Picnic 22). So keep an eye out for them. The sea churns up against the shelf, replenishing these pools: obviously, swimming isn't recommended in bad weather or when the sea is rough.

At **1h10min** spot a sea-shelf (from the edge of the plain) with a number of pools embedded in it. A few minutes' scrambling over rocks and boulders brings you down to them. This is an excellent spot for children, and the pools are also deep enough for adults. Some eight minutes later, there is another vast shelf with more inviting pools. Finally, a few minutes past this spot, you will find a magnificent solitary pool. All of these emerald-green waterholes are simply irresistible…

Attention is needed at about **2h10min**: shortly after turning inland (behind a small 'dip') to avoid a mass of lava rock, you pass a round WHITE CONCRETE TRIG MARKER that stands on a point to your right. Here you scramble over all the rock, to the top of the cliffs, for a dramatic coastal overlook. Two inviting green pools lie in what appears to be an inaccessible shelf, immediately below. Behind the pools stands an enormous cave — **El Convento** — with a 'cloistered' entrance opening back into the face of the cliff. A smaller cave sits to its right. Now the problem is: how do you get there?

The safest way down is just beyond the second cave, some four to five minutes round the top of the cliff. You pass over some interesting rock formations, resembling large fragments of broken crockery. Straight off this area of rock, you drop down onto 'lumps' of lava. Metres to the right (and close to the edge of the cliff!), a nose of rock reveals itself. Locating it requires a bit of scouting about. Descend here *with care!* All fours are needed, and this descent is only recommended for very sure-footed walkers! Also note: before venturing down, make sure the breakers aren't crashing over the shelf! When the sea is calm, there is no danger.

This is a superb and sheltered spot at which to spend the rest of the day. A BLOW HOLE lies a further 20 minutes along the coast, if you can summon up the energy. It's more noticeable for its noise than the spray of water. Find it on a sea-shelf set in the 'U' of the next bay along. The noise gives it away.

The return section of the walk is much easier on the feet: you follow a track that lies just a few minutes back from the top of the cliff — slightly inland from the path. Heading back, you get a good view of the Golfo crater — a prominent orange-coloured cone that rises up off the seashore. Remain on the track, keeping along the coast. Ignore all turn-offs inland. You'll cross several other tracks. By **3h** you should be passing the DESALINATION PLANT, where you cross the asphalt road leading to the LZ701. From here on no clear track is visible unless you go back closer to the coast. Just before the beach track you'll be traipsing across a rocky hillside. Above the **Playa de Janubio**, continue up the track to the right and, on the main road, turn left to the **La Hoya** junction and your BUS STOP (**3h45min**).

Rock pools (charcos) *lie all along the route, and make delightful swimming holes, many of them suitable for children.*

Walk 23: MONTAÑA CORONA (COSTA TEGUISE)

Distance: 8km/5mi; 2h30min-3h

Grade: moderate, with an ascent/descent of 235m/770ft. But you must be sure-footed and have a head for heights: paths are skiddy underfoot, and the crater rim may prove unnerving for some *(avoid very windy days)*.

Equipment: walking boots, fleece, sunhat, suncream

How to get there and return: 🚌 (Timetables 1, 9; alight at the 'Hotel Salinas' stop) or 🚗 to/from Costa Teguise (see map for parking places)

Less famous than its namesake near Máguez, Montaña Corona on the northern outskirts of Costa Teguise affords a wonderful 360° panorama from the top, stretching from the mountains in the north of the island all the way across the strait to Fuerteventura. It's a typical crescent-shaped volcano, with the side towards the sea missing. So the sure of foot can climb one arm of the arc, stride along the ridge, and descend by the other arm.

Begin in **Costa Teguise**: take CALLE DE LA ATALAYA which rounds the north side of the large, isolated HOTEL BEATRIZ. (You can cut through to it on a walkway 150m/ yds east of the bus stop; see map.) At the highest point of Calle de la Atalaya, before it bends left at the foot of the mountain, fork right on a ROUGH TRACK (**35min**) heading towards the main peak. Ignoring a path off right, aim for the BIG GAP IN THE CORNER OF THE DRYSTONE WALL ahead. Keep on the clear path through the gap and past a LARGE CAIRN (**42min**). After a further 100m/yds a path crosses, and a steep path goes straight ahead up the mountain's southern arm, to the summit.

This southerly path is not only steep but gravelly, so it is certainly easier going up than coming down, and most guides suggest ascending here. But I prefer to *turn right* here. My path, to the right, stays level for a bit, then dips into a little corrie. It carries you to the start of the north-eastern arm of the crescent. The sharp left turn leading up to the ridge is indicated by another large CAIRN. Now just climb the ridge, *stopping* to admire the views over the wild coastline and the odd bits of plant life somehow clinging to life in the cindery rubble.

The view from the TOP OF THE RIDGE is splendid — encompassing volcanic cones near and far, the distant wind generators to the north, the green 'sausages' of the golf course sitting in the gravy-brown lava, the massive network of drystone walls, and the white villages and specks of farmhouses. Arrecife, with its dominant power station, seems only a stone's throw away.

Curving along the ridge is reasonably easy in calm weather, but on windy days it may be wiser to keep below

114

Approaching the wall at the start of the climb

the highest part of the ridge, on the leeward side. The 'high point' of the walk, literally and metaphorically, is the southern end of the crescent, the SUMMIT of **Montaña Corona** (235m/770ft; **1h 30min**). From here you can see the myriad of paths that lead back into Costa Teguise, and you have several choices for the descent.

You *could* just plunge straight back down to the GAP in the wall. There is no path at first, but the way is mostly over bedrock. Lower down it's gravelly and skiddy: keep to the right here, where you will find more stable bedrock. You can be back in **Costa Teguise** in less than an hour (**2h30min**). Less steep descents will take longer: you could go back the way you came — or start back the way you came then, just before the CAIRN on the northeastern arm, *either* dive straight down (skiddy) *or fork due north* on a path for just 100m/yds, then fork right on another, gentler descent path which joins the more direct trail at another CAIRN. From here see the map: two right turns, followed by a left, would take you back to the Hotel Beatriz. Yet another option is to take the faint path down the west side of Corona (facing the golf course) and, at the bottom, fork left to get back to the CAIRN at the 42min-point.

Walk 24: TIMANFAYA — THE TERMESANA ROUTE

Distance: 3km/2mi; 2h walking (but allow about 4h)

Grade: easy, level walk

Equipment: stout shoes, fleece, raingear, sunhat, suncream

How to get there and return: 🚍 to/from the Timanfaya Visitors' Centre, just west of Mancha Blanca on the LZ67

Note: this is a guided walk and must be booked in advance **and reconfirmed** 24 hours before the date arranged. During Christmas, Easter and summer holidays it is wise to book at least *one or two months* in advance at www.reservasparquesnacionales.es (English pages). At other times, book before you travel to the island. At time of writing, children under 16 years of age were not allowed, even in the company of adults, so check in advance to avoid disappointment.

There's only one walk you can do in Timanfaya on your own — the coastal path north of El Golfo to Playa de la Madera (see page 123). But this doesn't take you into the heart of the volcanoes. *Do* try to do this walk — and as early in your visit as possible. You will learn so much that will add to the pleasure of the rest of your stay — after you have learned to 'read' the landscape. Not only are the guides schooled in vulcanology, but they can answer many more questions besides!

You may wonder why visitors are not allowed to walk freely in Timanfaya. There are several reasons. Firstly, some of the lava 'tunnels' have a very thin crust — your weight could collapse them, leading to a nasty accident, far from help. A second reason is a matter of aesthetics! The park is picture-postcard perfect: the rolling volcanic slopes all appear to be dusted with a smooth coating of caster sugar — a *pâtisserie* of pristine, freshly-iced cakes. But just one footprint in this sand changes its colour, and can take three years to disappear! It would take the wind

It's exhilarating to enter the national park on a clear day, when the Fire Mountains glow red above the sea of jagged 'AA' lava.

hundreds of years to smooth out jeep tracks. But the single most important reason is conservation. It can take lichen — the first of the vegetation, on which all subsequent growth depends, up to *900 years* to take hold. (Timanfaya is one of the best areas in the world to study lichens: they can be seen evolving on the naked rock in extreme conditions of heat and cold, their only source of moisture the water in the rock itself and the humidity of the northeast trade winds.) Some tiny lichen which you might not even notice bear hairs that provide life-giving moisture to the animals and birds which survive in the park. Lichens grow most readily on relatively flat surfaces (where they can trap the greatest amount of moisture; see photograph page 120) and in the crevices of northeast-facing slopes, where they catch the moisture off the trade winds.

Your day starts by assembling at the **Visitors' Centre** at 10 o'clock. The maximum group size is seven people, and usually there are two groups. Each starts at one end of this linear trail, and the drivers exchange minibus keys halfway along the walk. (In the rare case where there is only one group, you will do only half the walk — or, if you are all strong walkers, you will do the entire route and return the same way — 6km; your guide will decide which is best.) On the outward or inward trip, you will

travel via Yaiza, where your guide will point out two old houses that survived almost six years of eruptions beginning between nine and ten o'clock at night on September 1st, 1730. (Nearby is a raised water tank with a large tilted 'apron' surface to collect the water — a *mareta*. The actual tank below is much smaller than the 'apron'. These are less common than the *aljibes* — sunken water tanks with flat roofs.

How could some houses have survived and, more surprisingly, why was no one killed in the eruptions that obliterated 14 villages in what once was one of the most fertile areas on the island? Probably because the first material vomited out was 'AA' lava, which moves very slowly; families were able to load up their camels and get away. In an eruption, three types of lava spew out: *lapilli* (fine ash), *malpais* or AA type lava (scoria), and 'bombs'. Bombs are solid and hard; they fly on average 30 to 300km away from the volcano. Bombs can be tiny (you'll be given one to examine) or huge.

If you **start the walk** from the **Yaiza** (east) end of the trail, **Termesana** will be the first volcano you come to. You will see many fig trees here, most of them encircled by drystone lava walls. All this land was once private; now the national park has an arrangement with the farmers: the trees remain in private hands, but the farmers are obliged to use certain paths to reach their plots. The venerable old fig tree in the photograph on page 121 has a circumference of 12m — almost 40ft!

A very strange construction stands near the fig trees: a scoria-walled enclosure with a 3ft-high 'bed' of *lapilli* on top. What on earth could it be? Called a *pasero,* it's for drying the figs. Since scoria is full of holes, air can circulate all round the fruit. And on the subject of lava walls... those in this part of the park were built about 100 years ago by the men who built the walls in the Salinas de Janubio — 'master stonemasons', who can build a fairly high drystone wall using just one thickness of rock. (Try it yourself on one of your other walks — goodness knows but there's plenty of rock around to play with...)

The colours in the rocks are dazzling. And they vary enormously depending on their mineral content. Red comes as no surprise, but the sapphire-blue to mauve hues are particularly striking. Look at an example, as in the

photograph on page 120: you're likely to see that one part of the rock has been formed beneath the earth and another has been formed in contact with the air — this is often evident from the shape. The part that solidified underground comes out almost black, but the part that came into contact with the air is more red from oxidisation. Some rocks are blue from cobalt mixing with oxygen and others gold from sulphur. (The guides even claim to know which way the wind was blowing during the eruption, from the colour of the hillsides! They are likely to point out a cone with yellow streaking on only one side — indicating both the wind direction *and* a second passage of sulphurous wind as the rock cooled, which makes the gold colour even paler.)

Caldera Rajada ('Split Mountain') lies north of Termesana. If you thought volcanoes always 'blew their *tops*', then this one comes as a surprise. It split its *side*, and the resulting volcanic tube *(jameo)* reaches out just to the edge of your path. When tongues of lava flow from the point of eruption, they drag along the surface of the ground. The surface lava cools rapidly and solidifies, but molten lava (magma) continues to flow beneath the crust. The magma sinks gradually (either because the eruption ceases or because the flow follows a natural depression). Thus a cavity or 'tube' sometimes forms beneath the crust and the depressed lava flow (see photograph page 120). Volcanic tubes vary in size — this tube from Rajada formed inside and over a *barranco* and is very high. The ceilings of tubes vary greatly in thickness, too: some are very thick, while if you tap the tops of others, you'll hear how hollow they are! (At the end of the walk you'll climb

Top: the vivid colours in the rocks are due oxidation. Middle and bottom: it's easy to recognise the difference between jagged AA (malpais) *and* smooth pahoehoe lava. One type of pahoehoe lava is called 'ropey' for obvious reasons (middle). The solidified crusts of pahoehoe *lava* eventually break up into great blocks, sometimes revealing the underlying tubes.

inside a tube and see the 'stalactites', where the lava dripped as it cooled.) The famous tubes at the Cueva de los Verdes and Jameos del Agua resulted from the eruptions of Monte Corona (Walk 5).

Near the end of the walk you pass **Montaña Encantada** ('Enchanted Mountain') ... a cartographic misnomer. The fig farmers in the area paid a watchman to sit atop this mountain and sing out *('Canta!')* if anyone was stealing their fruit, so the mountain became known

Top: this massive fig tree at the foot of Montaña Termesana is still privately farmed: an arrangement between the park authorities and the owners of the land permits them to work their plots, but they must use agreed paths. Middle: after a long day carrying tourists, these camels are making their way home via Yaiza. Bottom: silky-sided craters rise from a sea of jagged scoria.

locally as Montaña Canta. But the map makers were from Madrid… Around here you will pass terrain where *malpais* and *pahoehoe* lava intermingle; their different surfaces make them instantly recognisable. There's a 'bubble' on show, too: called a *hornito*. You'll see other *hornitos* at César Manrique's house in Tahiche or if you do the walk around Lobos (see page 132). The walk ends at **Pedro Perico**, from where you take a minibus back to the **Visitors' Centre**.

COASTAL WALKS

My favourite coastal walks are described in full in the book, but there are many others to be enjoyed — especially if you can arrange transport, since most are linear. Here's a selection, with approximate walking times, grades and suggestions for access. If they are shown on a large-scale walking map, the page reference is given, but you really won't need a map beyond the touring map — just follow the coast and use common sense when you encounter property or a *barranco* to be negotiated. With the good coastal breezes, these hikes can even be done in summer, but *there is no shade: always* wear protective suncream and clothing (as well as stout lace-up shoes), and take plenty of water! Clockwise from Orzola:

Walk 25: SHORT WALK FROM ORZOLA
Distance: up to 2.5km/1.5mi; 50min
Grade: easy
Transport: 🚌 (Timetable 8) or 🚗 to/from Orzola

From the **Orzola** ferry terminal, walk up the coastal road to the left. When it ends, follow sandy tracks through the lava, heading diagonally towards the cliffs. When you approach **Playa de la Cantería**, you will see the old cliff path to Punta Fariones ahead. Follow it a short way, until you are above the far end of the beach (not far beyond here the path has fallen into the sea due to landslides).

Walk 26: LOS COCOTEROS TO COSTA TEGUISE
Distance: 9km/5.5mi; 2h30
Grade: moderate, with ups and downs of about 180m/590ft overall; you must be sure-footed
Transport: 🚌 (Timetables 1, 9) or 🚗 to/from Costa Teguise; then 🚕 taxi from Costa Teguise to the salt pans at Los Cocoteros to begin. (If you're travelling by bus, you could take an Orzola-bound bus to start (Timetable 8), and walk some 2km down the road to the salt pans.

Ask the taxi driver to set you down just before the salt pans at **Los Cocoteros**, where the main road turns left to the *urbanización* and a wide earthen track goes straight ahead (south). Follow the track — later a wide path — back to the Avenida de las Islas Canarias at **Costa Teguise** (map page 115).

Walk 27: PLAYA QUEMADA TO PUERTO DEL CARMEN
Distance: 6km/3.7mi; 2h
Grade: fairly easy; minimal ups and downs; **map** on pages 84-85

Transport: 🚌 (Timetables 1, 2, 12) or 🚗 to/from Puerto del Carmen; then 🚕 taxi from Puerto del Carmen to Playa Quemada to begin

Follow the road behind the seaside houses at **Playa Quemada**, heading towards Puerto Calero, then pick up a track running along the coast. By the first hotel in **Puerto Calero** (45min) take steps down to a private beach and back up again. Now follow the coastal promenade above the marina. When it ends at a gate, continue on a coastal path. Shortly before Puerto del Carmen a sometimes-stepped path

The lighthouses at Pechiguera

122

Walk 3: A greenery-bound farm against the sweep of the Famara cliffs

takes you down and across the **Barranco del Quiquere**. Then continue on the manicured path shown on page 84 and finally down a zigzag descent into **Puerto del Carmen**.

Walk 28: FARO PARK TO LA HOYA

Distance: 11km/6.8mi; 3.5-4h
Grade: fairly easy; **map** on page 110-111
Transport: 🚐 (Timetables 5, 12) or 🚐 to/from Playa Blanca, then 🚐 (Line 30, see box at the bottom of page 9) to the Faro Park development at the west end of Playa Blanca to start. Return on 🚐 from La Hoya (Playa Blanca bus, Timetable 5)

From the bus stop at **Faro Park** (map page 110-111) walk the short way west to a coastal track. Follow this north to an isolated house. At the end of the wall curving behind the house, you pick up a trail which soon widens to a track and passes another house. When you reach the abandoned *urbanización* Atlante del Sol (currently just a large, ugly, isolated ruin), you are just south of Walk 22. From here you can follow the track or the coastal path shown on the map.

Coast at Orzola (Walk 25)

Walk 29: CIRCUIT FROM EL GOLFO

Distance: 7km/4.3mi; 2h

Grade: easy-moderate ups and downs of 100m/330ft overall; volcanic rock underfoot throughout (boots *essential*). **Map** on pages 118-119.

Transport: 🚌 to El Golfo. Follow the coastal road through the village to the very end, by a parking area and childrens' playground.

Straight off the parking area, follow the coastal path north (usually edged with stones and easily seen). It merges with the southbound path from Playa de la Madera (Walk 30) at the point where a track crosses. Follow the track down left to **Playa del Paso**, a little-visited black sand beach. Then follow the track inland, past a couple of houses below **Montaña Quemada**, and take the next right turn. Past the last house, when this track heads south to the road, take the footpath straight ahead, back to the car park at **El Golfo**. *See also shorter version in the panel on page 32.*

Walk 30: PLAYA DE LA MADERA TO EL GOLFO

Distance: 13km/8mi; 5-6h

Grade: fairly strenuous due to length; volcanic rock underfoot throughout (boots *essential*). End of the walk on the **map** pages 118-119.

Transport: 🚌 Ask friends to take you to Playa de la Madera to start out and collect you at El Golfo. Otherwise, do Walk 29!

*This (and a short stretch of Walk 29) are the only parts of the Timanfaya National Park where you can walk without a guide, but you are asked **not** to venture off the made path.* The path leaves from the far side of **Playa de la Madera**. The rock formations and the constant breaking of the waves are an endless source of enjoyment, and you have the backdrop of Timanfaya all along the route (photograph page 78). Just before **Playa del Paso**, cross a track and continue on the path into **El Golfo**.

Walk 31: CIRCUIT FROM LA CALETA DE FAMARA

Distance: 16km/10mi; 4h30min-5h

Grade: moderate but long; overall ascents about 200m/560ft; the tracks/paths shift under sand *(avoid windy days!)*, but orientation is easy.

Transport: 🚌 or 🚐 (Timetables 13, 14) to/from La Caleta de Famara. By car or on foot go through La Caleta and out on a 'dual carriageway' track to Playa de San Juan; motorists can park here, saving 2.5km return.

Shifting sands make this is a walk for those who are very relaxed about where they end up and when they get there! It was suggested by readers; Sunflower has *not* checked the whole route. From the beach, walk back and take the first right for 'Dominique'. Ignore 'private' signs and go straight through the Bajamar development, ignoring the right turn to Villa Dominique. You can see your path up the first volcano: make your way fairly steeply to the top. From the rim enjoy the terrific view to the Famara cliffs, then locate a T-junction in the tracks below (due north). Continue round the rim to a depression where a path goes down to the plain. Walk to the T-junction and take the track/path heading west to the next volcano. Follow the trail right to the top of the volcano and round the rim until it descends back in the direction from which you came. But abruptly the trail makes a U-turn and heads west again. Although it is often obscured by sand, you should be able to follow this path as it reaches and then skirts a third volcano. It then continues more clearly up to the fourth, final volcano, just north of Sóo. A track leads to the edge of the crater, where a short but steep climb (no path) takes you to the northern rim and the most fantastic view to the mountains of the national park, to La Santa and round to Famara. Rejoin the track and head seaward. By turning right, the track would take you all the way back to Caleta. Or just walk along the top of the beach.

A day out on
Fuerteventura

*The numbers on this touring map indicate car tours and walks in the
book *Landscapes of Fuerteventura*.

Car tour 3: A DAY OUT ON FUERTEVENTURA

Playa Blanca • Corralejo • Dunes Natural Park • (Puerto del Rosario) • Caleta de Fuste • Antigua • Tuineje • Pájara • Puerto de la Peña • Betancuria • La Oliva • (El Cotillo) • Lajares • Corralejo • Playa Blanca

190km/118mi; 6 hours driving (plus 12min each way on the ferry and any driving on Lanzarote to reach Playa Blanca)

On route: Picnic by the Presa de las Peñitas, or have lunch at Pájara.

*This is a **very** long day. **Do** plan on taking the first ferry in the morning and returning on the last one. There is no need to pre-book; just turn up about half an hour before sailing time and buy your tickets at the office on the pier at Playa Blanca. Either fill up with petrol at the roundabout just outside Playa Blanca, or in Corralejo. This tour takes in the sights of the north and middle of Fuerteventura — it's just not practicable to get to the Jandía Peninsula as well on a day trip from Lanzarote. To visit Jandía, you should spend at least one night on the island. Puerto del Rosario, the capital, is only included as an optional detour — I concentrate on the **countryside**. Roads are all good, but the road between Pájara and the Vega de Río de Palmas is narrow, with very sheer drops; it is built up at the side, but some motorists might find it unnerving. See map of northern Fuerteventura and plan of Corralejo on the reverse of the Lanzarote touring map inside the back cover.*

Get up with the birds to make the most of this day — not only to get value from the cost of your ferry crossing, but to take in the best landscapes. After spending a week or so on Lanzarote, Fuerteventura comes as a bit of a shock! Lanzarote's landscapes are so neatly-manicured, so bright-white, so *tidy*. Corralejo, by contrast, looks ramshackle and dusty as you bump your way off the ferry. And Fuerteventura's landscapes are equally unkempt. You'll drive for miles and miles with hardly a sign of habitation — just rosy-red untamed hillsides, dotted with the odd palm or windmill. And when you *do* come upon settlements, you may be delighted to find a wealth of old buildings full of character and colour ... even though some of them appear to be coming apart at the seams.

Leave Corralejo's port following signs for 'Puerto del Rosario' and 'Las Playas'. Joining the coastal road to Puerto del Rosario (FV1), you head out through the **Dunes Natural Park★** — white caster-sugar sands stretching as far as the eye can see. This stunning stretch of white shimmering sand is further enhanced by the aquamarine sea and the purply-blue hills that rise in the background. Lobos (Walk 32) stands out clearly on your left, offshore, with its hundreds of little hillocks and guardian volcano. The dunes are supposedly a natural park, but all the same, a couple of hotels interrupt this unique stretch of beauty (⏷ ✕).

Out of this mini-desert, you cross a featureless stone-littered plain. At 19km pass a turn-off to Parque Holandés

126

The Dunes Natural Park near Corralejo

(▲✕): a number of tourist booklets recommend a visit, but I would advise you to skip it. This tour also bypasses Puerto del Rosario (▲▲▲✕✝♥⊕M); the town centre has little to offer the passing tourist. So on your approach to the capital, keep following 'aeropuerto', to stay on the ring road, the FV3. Watch for your turn-off: filter right for 'aeropuerto' and 'Morro Jable' (37.5km): this takes you back to the coastal road (FV2 ♥) and you pass a hotel on the left at 39km (▲▲).

Caleta de Fuste (▲▲▲✕⊕) is a popular tourist centre. To see the best (older) part of it, take the *second* turn-off, signposted 'Puerto Castillo'. A beautiful palm-lined road takes you to the circular 18th-century defense tower (El Castillo) by the little yachting harbour.

Return to the main road and continue south. At 65km turn right for Antigua on the FV50. On coming to a main road (FV20; ♥) turn right again, into **Antigua** (74km ✝ ▲▲✕). The square is beautifully laid out; the church simple but imposing nevertheless. Just north of Antigua on the FV20 (the Puerto del Rosario road) stands **El Molino★** (✕), a well-preserved 200-year-old windmill, once used for grinding corn, now a handicraft centre. The windmill is an appropriate introduction to Antigua, because this area has the highest concentration of windmills on Fuerteventura — as you will see as you head south towards Tuineje on the FV20.

Out in the country again, palms return to the scene. A trickle of villages is seen sitting back in the plain. Threading your way through hills, you find cultivated fields sheltering along the floors of the *barrancos*. You pass some photogenic windmills on your route through **Valles de**

Ortega, **Agua de Bueyes** and **Tiscamanita** (✕ and small windmill information centre, 'Centro de Interpretación Los Molinos'). Three dark volcanoes, La Laguna, Liria and Los Arrabales, rupture the lake of lava that spills out over the plains on your left. This area is called the *malpais* ('badlands'). Around **Tuineje** (86km 🚌) the large *fincas* of the tomato-growers stand out in the barren landscape.

Head out right on the FV30 towards Pájara. Rosy-rusty tones emanate from the landscape and are reflected in the honey-coloured stone of the walls and old ruins. You cross a col and a huge basin opens up ahead, with views to the sea. Down in the valley, on the approach to **Toto**, you'll spot 'wigwams' of cane, waiting to be used in the tomato fields. **Pájara** (94km ✝ ▲▲ ✕ and swimming pool) is a large farming community surrounded by hills. The shady village is a welcoming sight, with its abundance of trees and small colourful gardens. Don't miss the church here; it is especially noteworthy for the striking 'Aztec' stone-carved decoration above the main entrance. Quite a curiosity because, apart from similar sculptures in La Oliva, these carvings are unique in the Canaries. The two naves inside the church date back to 1645 and 1687, while the carving over the door is thought to date from the 1500s. If you haven't brought a picnic, nearby Casa Isaítas (a *hotel rural*) serves good home cooking.

From Pájara take the FV621, to descend to Ajuy/ Puerto de la Peña. Rounding a corner, you look down into a valley lush with palm trees, tamarisk shrubs and

Betancuria

garden plots. Below **Ajuy** you come into **Puerto de la Peña** (103km), a small village set on the edge of a black sand beach. It's one of two fishing settlements on the west coast. Few tourists venture over to the dramatically-sited ancient port here. It hides in a bay some 15 minutes' walk around the coast to the south of the village.

From Puerto de la Peña return to Pájara, then take the road for Vega de Río Palmas (FV30, signposted for Betancuria); it's at the left of the church. Again you ascend into the hills, climbing on a narrow winding road that hugs the sheer inclines (some people might find this road unnerving). There are excellent views back over the Barranco de Pájara. The Degollada de los Granadillos (☞) is the pass that takes you over a solid spur of rock that juts out into the valley below. From here you have a superb outlook over to the enclosing rocky ridges.

Soon, descending, you come to a another large parking area overlooking the **Presa de las Peñitas** (☞), a muddy reservoir lodged in the V of the Barranco de las Peñitas. The reservoir looks deeper than it is, as it has filled with silt; in summer it's bone dry. Groves of tamarisk trees huddle around the tail of the presa, and that's a good spot from which to do some bird-watching. Green gardens step the sides of the slopes, and palm trees complement the scene. Below the reservoir lies a sheer-sided rocky ravine, the ideal hiding place for the chapel dedicated to the island's patron saint, Nuestra Señora de la Peña.

This impressive ravine is one of the island's beauty spots, so let's do more exploring. Past the viewpoint, the rest of the valley opens up, and a string of *casas* stretches along it. They're set amidst a healthy sprinkling of palms and cultivated plots — a luxuriant corner. Turn down *sharp* left at the first road you come to, just before the centre of **Vega de Río Palmas**. This 3km-long road is very narrow, but there is room for two cars to pass. Continue to a turning area at the end of the road. This is an exquisite picnic spot beside the reservoir, with shady palms and a symphony of birdsong.

Return to the main road, pass the church dedicated to Nuestra Señora de la Peña on the right, and continue twisting up the valley. The countryside subsides into rolling contours once again. Notice a large abandoned field of sisal on the hillsides on your left, a short distance further on. This crop was introduced from Mexico.

At the end of this valley you come to the village of **Betancuria**★ (134km ✠♠✕M), well hidden from the

marauding Berbers of earlier centuries. It's a very picturesque collection of manorial buildings, with a grand
17th-century cathedral. The cathedral and convent here
are the oldest examples of their style in the archipelago.
Relics abound in historic Betancuria, and I hope you'll
notice some of them. A number of the old houses have
doorways and arches dating back to the 15th century.
Betancuria was the capital of Fuerteventura for some 400
years, up until 1835, and was also the first episcopal seat
for all the Canaries. The oldest part of the village huddles
around the cathedral. History-hunters will enjoy the
cathedral and the small Museo Sacreo here — as well as
the municipal museum.

Leaving Betancuria on the FV30, everyone passes by
the Franciscan monastery, the shell of which sits below
the road on the northern side of the village. Inside it
(unseen from the road) are some beautiful cloistered
arches. Near the convent is a small enclosed church —
actually the first church on the island; however, much of
the building was rebuilt in the 17th century.

You zigzag up out of the valley and pull over at the
top of the pass (📷) for a fine panorama over a vast plain
to the north. Its far-distant reaches are edged by sharp
abrupt hills called *cuchillos* (knives); over on your left lie
morros (low, smooth hills). Betancuria nestles cosily in the
valley floor below.

Leaving the viewpoint, when you come to a roundabout, turn left. Pass through **Valle de Santa Inés** and
Llanos de la Concepción. At another roundabout go left
for 'Tefía, La Oliva' (FV207). After passing between
Montaña Bermeja on the left and Morro Bermejo on the
right, mellow old stone walls and farmhouses introduce
Tefía (**M**). Beyond the village, turn left on the FV10 for
La Oliva. You next pass above **Tindaya** (✗). It spreads
across a flattened crest amidst a profusion of faded brown
stone walls. Behind the village stands captivating
Montaña Tindaya, a great rocky salient that dominates
the surrounding countryside with its boldness. Perhaps
this is why the Guanches chose it as their holy mountain.

At the other end of this plain lies the pleasant country
village of **La Oliva**★ (166km ⚕▲✗🏠M). It rests on the
edge of a lava flow. Montaña Arena, a mountain of sand,
rises up out of the lava in the background. Drive straight
ahead to the church, where there's ample parking. Nuestra
Señora de Candelaria overpowers the village with its solid
black-stone belfry. La Oliva was a town of some impor-

tance in the 17th century, when the island's military post was stationed here. The official residence (the Colonels' House, open Tue-Sat, 10.00-18.00, entrance fee) can be seen on the outskirts of the village: follow signs for 'Casa de los Coroneles' and 'Centro de Arte Canario'. The Centro de Arte Canario (Casa Mané; **M**), a museum of contemporary Canarian art, is well worth a visit. One can't help but notice the perfectly-shaped Montaña Frontón rising up in the background of this naked setting; in fact, it's not a real mountain, but only the tail of a long ridge. The Casa del Capellán (Chaplain's House), another old and dilapidated building, sits off the side of the Corralejo road, on the left. This house, and a small house in the village, which has a stone façade with an Aztec motif, are other examples of the as yet unexplained Mexican influence seen earlier in the day at Pájara.

From La Oliva make for Lajares: take the road forking left opposite the church, towards 'El Cotillo'. The road runs alongside the pale green lichen-smeared *malpais* — a pleasant change in the landscape. Bear right for Lajares where the main road goes left to El Cotillo.*

You circle Montaña La Arena before coming into **Lajares** (177km) and passing between two roadside windmills. The one on your left is called a *molina:* a wooden contraption that rotates and is built onto the rooftop of a house. The house normally has a room on either side of the mill. On your right is a *molino:* it's conical and is rotated by pushing the long arms, thus moving the cap with the windmill blades. This building is not inhabited. Both mills were used for grinding *gofio*. There's also a curious church nearby. Lajares is an attractive little village of white houses set amidst dark lava-stone walls.

From here it's a straightforward run back to Corralejo: turn right at the roundabout in Lajares, taking the FV109, then turn left on the FV101 at a T-junction. (A right turn here would take you back towards Villaverde and La Oliva. Just before Villaverde, the museum and volcanic tube of Cueva del Llano, open daily from 10.00-18.00, is well worth a visit). You drive through *malpais* almost all the way to the outskirts of **Corralejo**, from where you follow a palm-lined dual carriageway back towards the port (190km).

*How are you doing for time till the last ferry? If possible, *do* make a 17km return detour to El Cotillo (🏔🏔⛺✕). Any of the tracks leading out past the 17th-century watchtower on the cliffs would give you a taste of the exquisite little coves ensconced in the dark lava coastline.

Walk 32: AROUND LOBOS

Distance: 10km/6.2mi; 2h45min

Grade: easy, but there is no shade, and it can be hot, windy and dusty. The ascent of Montaña La Caldera is just over 100m/330ft.

Equipment: comfortable walking shoes, fleece, sunhat, suncream, picnic, plenty of water, swimwear

How to get there and return: ⚓ 'Princesa Ico' (www.princesa-ico. com) excursion boat to Corralejo on Fuerteventura and Lobos. As this is fairly expensive, check in advance how many hours you will have on Lobos. *Note that this excursion only operates in summer.* In summer you *may* also be able to find a boat to take you to Lobos: enquire at the port in Playa Blanca. Or ⚓ from Corralejo to Lobos (Timetable 15).

You can have Fuerteventura's Jandía and El Jable; I'll settle for Lobos any day. A short — 2km from Corralejo or 8km from Playa Blanca — ferry ride takes you over to this strange little island of sand and rocky mounds. Seen from afar, it may not even arouse your curiosity. But once you've seen the exquisite lagoon cradled by Casas El Puertito and you've climbed the crater, then finished your day with a dip in the turquoise green waters off the shore, you'll remember it as one of the highlights of your holiday. Lobos takes its name from the seals that once inhabited these waters.

You follow a track that circles the island. A quad, which belongs to the park rangers, is the only vehicle you'll encounter. On Lobos all the paths and tracks are very clearly marked — *with signs warning you not to leave the marked route: Lobos is a bird sanctuary and a protected area!* Straight off the JETTY, **start out** by forking right twice and heading for the tiny port of Casas El Puertito, a jumble of buildings with a restaurant. A neat wide path leads you there through a landscape dominated by mounds of lava and littered with rock. These small mounds, called *hornitos* ('little ovens'; see page 134) are caused by phreatic eruptions. You'll see the beautiful *Limonium papillatum,* with its paper-like mauve and white flowers. And fluorescent green *tabaiba* glows amidst the sombre rock. You'll also notice plenty of *cosco (Mesembryanthemum nodiflorum),* the noticeably bright red ice plant, and *Suaeda vera.* A reef of rocky outcrops shelters the lagoon, making it into a perfect natural swimming pool. Through the rock you can see the sand dunes of Corralejo in the background; **Casas El Puertito** (**7min**) is a picture postcard setting. (Tip: if you want to eat here after your walk, order your meal now!)

Once past the little houses, you continue around the LAGOON. Almost at once, swing back inland and, at a T junction, head left. To the right is a coastal path: if you take it, you can rejoin the main walk once you reach the tidal pools.) *Arthrocnemum fruticosum* (a fern-like plant) grows in the hollows. Ice plants (see page 39), with transparent papillae resembling water droplets, also catch the attention. This plant was once traded for its soda content. The track loops its way through these miniature 'mountains'. The rock is clad in orange and faded-green lichen. Overlooking all this is Montaña La Caldera (the crater), the most prominent feature in this natural park.

Shortly, cross a sandy flat area. The track loops up the embankment; a small fork off to the left cuts the loop and joins the track at an INFORMATION BOARD. Lanzarote begins to grow across the horizon. Ignore the forks off to the right (**30min, 37min**). (The second fork leads past a patch of sisal — an aloe-like plant with exceptionally tall flower stems, sheltering in a hollow just a few minutes away.) Soon (**55min**), ignore side-paths to some ugly concrete buildings. Then join a track coming in from the left. In a few minutes you're alongside the abandoned building and outhouses of the **Faro de Martiño** (**1h10min**). If you don't plan to climb the crater, this will be your best viewpoint in the walk. You look out over the dark lava hills and the tiny valleys of golden sand that thread their way through them. To the right of the broken-away crater of Montaña La Caldera you'll glimpse Corralejo. Across the straits, just opposite, lie some of Lanzarote's magnificent beaches, from Playa Blanca to Punta Papagayo.

From the lighthouse follow the main track off to the right (the GR131). Within 30 minutes from the lighthouse (at about **1h40min**), you will turn off to climb Montaña La Caldera, by taking the *second* fork off to the right. But first you might like to take a 30 minute return detour to Caleta del Palo, a beach inside Montaña La Caldera's crater. If so, take the *first* right turn (where a signpost points forwards and backwards, but *not* to the Caleta del Palo) and follow the track along a sandy depression. *(Careful: in late spring and early summer breeding seagulls around here can be very aggressive!)* Pass a water tank and continue on a path through a narrow 'valley' of rock, which leads down to this black-sand beach. Return the same way.)

The **Montaña La Caldera** turn-off comes up four minutes after the detour route. Straight into this track, the route forks. Go right and follow the well-worn path that ascends to the RIM OF THE CRATER (**2h10min**). A

The 'hornitos' of Lobos — an intriguing landscape. These phreatic eruptions come about when underground water heats up and expands.

brilliant sight awaits you. You find yourself on a razor-sharp ridge, looking down sheer walls onto a beach, hidden inside this half-crater. Your vista encompasses the profusion of *hornitos* that make up this island, the dunes of Corralejo, and Fuerteventura's hazy inland hills. To the north, you can trace Lanzarote's coastline as far as Puerto del Carmen. The crater is also home to a large seagull colony. The birds here seem used to visitors, and not aggressive. Take time to observe the fascinating social behaviour of these beautiful and elegant birds.

Returning to the main track, head right. In 15 minutes, watch for the turn-off to the main beach: it comes up two minutes past two concrete buildings that sit in a hollow on your left. This exquisite bay (**Playa de la Concha; 2h 30min**) is a shallow lagoon that curves deeply back into the coastline. Here's where you'll end up passing the rest of the day, no doubt. Keep an eye on your boat's departure time! To return to the ferry, just continue along the track, keeping right at the fork, to the JETTY (**2h45min**).

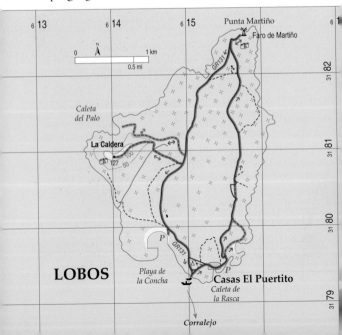

LOBOS

BUS AND FERRY TIMETABLES

Log on to www.intercitybuslanzarote.es (see page 7) for the latest timetables, or see ferry operators below

1: Arrecife–Costa Teguise (Line 1); 20min
Dep Arrecife *Mon–Fri:* 06.40 and approx every 20 min until 22.40, then 23.40; *Sat/Sun/hols:* 06.40 and twice-hourly at 10 and 40 past the hour until 23.40
Dep Costa Teguise *Mon–Fri:* 07.00 and every 20 min until 22.40, then 23.00, 00.10; *Sat/Sun/hols:*07.00 and every 30 min until 23.00, then 23.30, 00.10

2: Arrecife–Pto Carmen–Pto Calero (Line 2); 30min
Dep Arrecife *Mon–Fri:* 06.20 and every 20 min until 22.40, then 23.20; *Sat/Sun/hols:* 06.20 and at 20 and 50 min past the hour until 22.20, then 23.20
Dep Puerto del Carmen (buses leave **Puerto Calero** a few min earlier) *Mon–Fri:* 07.00 and every 20 min until 22.20, then 23.00, 00.10; *Sat/Sun:* 07.00, 08.00 and every 30 min until 23.00, then 00.10

3: Airport (Lines 22, 23); circular routes; 20min
Two *circular* routes between the capital and the airport on a *daily* basis, with frequent departures starting at 06.50 from Arrecife. Service is half-hourly after 08.00

4: Arrecife–Conil–La Asomada–Femés (Line 5); to Femés about 1h
Dep Arrecife *Mon–Fri only* 08.00, 14.00, 19.15
Dep Femés *Mon–Fri only* 09.00, 14.45, 19.15

5: Arrecife–Playa Honda–Tías–Macher–Uga–Yaiza–Playa Blanca† (Line 60); to Playa Blanca about 1h
Dep Arrecife *Mon–Fri:* 06.00+ and every hour on the hour until 21.00; *Sat/Sun/hols:*07.00, 08.00*, 09.00, 11.00, 13.00, 14.00*=, 15.00, 17.00, 19.00, 21.00
Dep Playa Blanca *Mon–Fri:* 06.50+, 07.00 and every hour on the hour until 22.00; *Sat/Sun/hols:*08.00, 09.00*=, 10.00, 12.00, 14.00, 15.00*, 16.00, 18.00, 20.00, 22.00

*only Sundays;+Line 06, via Puerto del Carmen; = Line 13
†See also box at the bottom of page 125

6: Arrecife–Teguise–Mala–Arrieta–Haría–Máguez† (Line 7); to Máguez about 1h
Dep Arrecife *Mon–Fri:* 08.00, 10.00, 12.30, 14.30, 16.30, 18.30=, 20.30; *Sat/Sun/hols:* 08.00, 10.00, 12.00, 14.00, 18.00, 20.00
Dep Máguez *Mon–Fri:* 07.00, 09.00, 11.00, 13.30, 15.30, 17.30, 19.30; *Sat/Sun/hols:* 07.00, 09.00, 11.00, 13.00, 19.00, 21.00
= goes on to Ye as Line 26

7: Arrecife–Teguise* (Los Valles bus, Line 10); to Teguise about 15-20min
Dep Arrecife *Mon–Fri: only (except holidays)* 06.30, 10.00=, 14.00=, 16.00=, 20.40=
Dep Teguise *Mon–Fri: only (except holidays)* 07.05, 10.35=, 14.35=, 16.35=, 21.15=
*Lines 11, 12, 13 serve Teguise (market) *on Sundays only;* check the website; = Line 26;

8: Arrecife–Orzola (Line 9); 45min
Dep Arrecife *Mon–Fri:* 07.40, 10.30, 12.00, 15.30, 17.00; *Sat/Sun/hols:* 07.40, 15.30, 17.00
Dep Orzola *Mon–Fri:* 08.30, 11.30, 13.10, 16.40, 18.10; *Sat/Sun/hols:* 08.30, 16.40, 18.10

9: Pto Carmen–Costa Teguise (Line 03); 20min
Dep Puerto del Carmen *Mon–Fri:* approx every 20 min from 07.00 until 21.40; *Sat/Sun/hols:* approx every 30 min from 10.00 until 21.00
Dep Costa Teguise *Mon–Fri:* approx every 20 min from 07.00 until 21.20; *Sat/Sun/hols:* approx every 20 min from 09.00 until 22.00

10: Arrecife–Pto Calero (Line 24); 25min
Dep Arrecife *Mon–Fri:* 07.00, 09.00, 11.20, 15.00, 19.40, 23.20; *Sat/Sun/hols:*07.20, 10.20, 11.50, 14.50, 19.50, 23.20
Dep Puerto Calero *Mon–Fri:* 07.30, 09.30, 11.50, 15.30, 20.10, 24.00; *Sat/Sun/hols:*07.50, 10.50, 12.20, 15.20, 20.20, 24.00

11: Arrecife–San Bartolomé–Tiagua–Tinajo —La Santa (Line 16); to Tinajo 25min
Dep Arrecife *Mon–Fri:* 07.00, 08.00, 09.00, 11.00=, 12.00+, 14.00+, 15.00=, 17.00=, 18.00+, 19.00, 21.10, 21.40=; *Sat/Sun/hols:* 08.00, 10.15, 12.00, 14.00, 15.45, 17.30, 19.00, 20.30
Dep La Santa *Mon–Fri:* 07.00, 08.00, 09.00=, 10.00+, 12.00+, 13.00=, 15.00=, 16.00+, 18.00, 19.00, 19.50=; *Sat/Sun/hols:* 07.00, 08.45, 11.00, 12.45, 14.45, 16.45, 18.15, 19.45
=Line 52; +Line 53

12: Puerto del Carmen–Playa Blanca= (Line 161); about 1h
Dep Puerto del Carmen* *Mon–Fri:* 06.20=, 07.30 and every hour on the half hour until 22.30; *Sat/Sun/hols:* 08.00 and every two hours on the hour until 22.00
Dep Playa Blanca*
Mon–Fri: 06.50, 08.30 and every hour on the half hour until 23.30; *Sat/Sun/hols:*09.00 and every two hours on the hour until 23.00
=See also box at the bottom of page 9 (Line 30)
*The bus actually starts at the airport before going into Puerto del Carmen; buses from Playa Blanca terminate at the airport.

13: Arrecife–Sóo–Caleta de Famara (Line 20); about 1h
Dep Arrecife *Mon–Fri: only* 06.30, 09.45, 14.00, 17.45, 20.45
Dep Caleta *Mon–Fri: only* 07.00, 08.40, 17.00, 20.45

14: Costa Teguise–Teguise–Caleta de Famara (Line 31); about 1h
Dep Costa Teguise *Mon–Fri:* 07.30=, 09.30=, 11.30, 13.00, 15.30=, 17.30, 19.30, 21.15; *Sat/Sun/hols:* 09.00, 11.00, 13.00, 15.00, 17.00, 19.00, 20.30
Dep Caleta *Mon–Fri:* 08.30=, 10.30=, 12.15, 13.45, 16.30=, 18.30, 20.30, 22.00; *Sat/Sun/hols:* 10.00, 12.00, 14.00, 16.00, 18.00, 19.45, 21.15
=Line 33

⚓ 15: Lobos boats (all daily from Corralejo on Fuerteventura); 35min
Isla de Los Lobos; *dep* 10.10; *ret* 16.00 or 18.00
El Majorero; *dep* 10.00, 12.00; *ret* 12.30, 16.00
Celia Cruz; *dep* 09.45; *ret* 14.20 or 17.00

⚓ 16: Bocayna Express (Fred Olsen Line; www.fredolsen.es) from Playa Blanca to Corralejo on Fuerteventura; 15min
Dep Playa Blanca *daily:* 07.10 (Mon–Fri only), 08.00, 10.00, 14.00, 16.00, 18.00
Dep Corralejo *daily:* 07.45+, 09.00, 11.00, 15.00, 17.00, 19.00

⚓ 17: Volcán de Tindaya (Armas Line; www.naviera-armas.com) from Playa Blanca to Corralejo on Fuerteventura; 40min
Dep Playa Blanca *daily:* 07.00, 09.00, 11.00, 15.00, 17.00, 19.00
Dep Corralejo *daily:* 08.00, 10.00, 14.00, 16.00, 18.00, 20.00

⚓ 18: Graciosa Ferry (from Orzola); (www.lineas romero.com); 25min
Dep Orzola *daily:* 10.00, 11.00, 12.00, 13.30, 16.00, 17.00, 18.00 (and 19.00 from 1 July to 1 October)
Dep Caleta del Sebo (Graciosa) *daily:* 08.00, 10.00, 11.00, 12.30, 15.00, 16.00, 17.00 (and 18.00 from 1 July to 1 October)

⚓ 19: Graciosa Ferry (from Orzola); (www.biosfera express.com); 25min
Dep Orzola *daily:* 07.00, 09.30, 10.30*, 11.30, 15.30, 16.30*, 17.30, 18.30*
Dep Caleta del Sebo (Graciosa) *daily:* 08.00, 10.00, 11.30*, 13.00, 16.30, 17.30*, 18.30, 19.30*
*summer only (1 July to 25 October)

135

● Index

Geographical names comprise the only entries in this index; for other entries see Contents, page 3. **Bold-face type** indicates a photograph; *italic type* indicates a map reference. Both may be in addition to a text reference on the same page.